THE
CHARM OF BIRDS

THE CHARM OF BIRDS LIBRARY

Book One

General Editor

Michael Waterhouse

THE
CHARM OF BIRDS

Sir Edward Grey

WOODCUTS BY ROBERT GIBBINGS

INTRODUCTION BY MICHAEL WATERHOUSE

Weidenfeld & Nicolson

LONDON

First published in Great Britain 1927 by Hodder and Stoughton
This edition published 2001 by Weidenfeld & Nicolson
an imprint of The Orion Publishing Group
Orion House, 5 Upper St Martin's Lane,
London WC2H 9EA

A CIP catalogue record for this book is available
from the British Library

ISBN 0 575 07058 7

Typeset by Selwood Systems, Midsomer Norton
Printed and bound in Great Britain by
Butler & Tanner Ltd, Frome and London

To Pamela

The editor would particularly like to thank Sir Edward Grey's great nephew, Mr Christopher Graves, for his agreement to publish *The Charm of Birds*.

CONTENTS

ʚɞ

PREFACE

ເ୨ເ୨

This book will have no scientific value. Those who have studied birds will not find in it anything that they do not already know; those who do not care for birds will not be interested in the subject. The writing of the book, and still more the publishing of it, require some explanation.

There are three categories of books about British birds for which the reason and justification are apparent:

1. Books of which the main purpose is to give coloured representations of each species; and thereby to enable us to recognise a bird by referring to the

picture of it. The work brought out by the late Lord Lilford is one example of this kind.

2. Manuals that collect and bring up to date what is known about every sort of British bird. These are invaluable; one at least should be available to everybody who studies birds: but like encyclopædias, these are for reference and not intended to be read through continuously from cover to cover. Seebohm, Howard Saunders and Coward are examples of this category. So are the volumes of Kirkman and Thorburn, which have coloured illustrations as well as being stores of information.

3. Books that are the outcome of personal observation by the writer of particular species or individual birds. Eliot Howard's books on the British Warblers, and on 'Territory', are fine examples of this category; and in it may also be placed articles, such as those of J. P. Burkitt in *British Birds* and in *The Irish Naturalist*, and of E. M. Nicholson recently in *The Field*. These are books or articles to be read right through. They are a most valuable contribution to our knowledge. They throw new light on territory, courtship, mating and the intimate life of birds.

Personal observation will always make a book valuable. In this book there will be some things here and there that may deserve to be placed in this last category, but they will be slight and not thorough. My opportunities for watching birds have been intermittent. My observations have been made for recreation; in search of pleasure, not of knowledge; and they have been pursued only in so far as they ministered to the pleasure of holidays and home life. Nevertheless the interest in wild birds that began in early manhood, continued. It provided one form of recreation that was increasingly satisfactory, and it is pleasant to pay a tribute to the interest and pleasure that birds have given. One who reviews pleasant experiences and puts them on record increases the value of them to himself; he gathers up his own feelings and reflections, and is thereby better able to understand and to measure the fullness of what he has enjoyed. This may account sufficiently for the impulse to write; but it is not relevant to the question of publication, and on this point there are one or two things to be said.

When I was beginning to notice birds I found delight and help in Warde Fowler's *A Year with the Birds*. Here was a man whose work – he was a Don at Oxford – had, like my own, lain outside study of Natural History. He had been doing for many years with birds just what I was beginning to do: he had found it a pleasant path for recreation. This book of his did, as it were, blaze a trail, which any one with an inclination to birds could follow, and thereby be led to find much pleasure. This book of mine may perhaps be of some use in the same manner.

After all, it is not entirely to exchange information that lovers of birds converse together on this subject. An artist will paint the commonest object in order to bring out some aspect that has particularly struck him. So with watchers of birds, some are attracted by one aspect of a well-known species and some by another. Thus even those of us who have nothing new to tell, may have something that is fresh to say.

INTRODUCTION

Michael Waterhouse

Sir Edward Grey, Viscount Grey of Fallodon, was one of the most interesting and accomplished Englishmen of the late nineteenth and early twentieth centuries, at one and the same time parliamentarian, statesman, railwayman, countryman, pioneer conservationist and author. He is nevertheless best remembered for his words, spoken as Foreign Secretary at the outbreak of the First World War: 'The lights are going out all over Europe. We shall not see them lit again in our lifetime.'

Grey entered Parliament in 1885 as Liberal Member for Berwick-upon-Tweed. If the prerequisite to becoming a great Parliamentarian is an ability to hold the floor of the House, then Edward Grey was one of a dying breed. In Grey's time it was difficult, indeed almost impossible, to reach the peaks in political life without having such authority, and it appears that Grey acquired these gifts early in his career. In the spring of 1895 rumours abounded of a French expedition from West Africa across the continent to the headwaters of the Nile. Grey, in his capacity as Under Secretary of State for Foreign Affairs, informed the House in determined terms that such action would be considered unfriendly. Shortly after 'Grey's Declaration', Prime Minister Lord Rosebery said, 'Grey is *persona gratissima* to the House of Commons, popular, admired and respected.' Grey impressed the House not by the sharpness of his intellect or the brilliance of his speech but by his sound grasp of fact and the simple sincerity of his tone. There were no theatricals in his delivery, no emotion in his voice; it was always a cool impassive delivery. He was without exception calm, dignified, sound, temperate and strong. He was also assisted by his patrician good looks – a distinctive clean-shaven appearance.

Later in Grey's career, whenever there was a tricky debate in the House, Asquith would call on his Foreign Secretary to conclude proceedings. The most dramatic episode took place in July 1911 when the Lords' amendments to the Parliament Bill were sent back to the House. Asquith was howled down for a full thirty minutes. Margot Asquith was present in the Ladies Gallery and sent a note down to Grey on the floor of the House: 'They will listen to you so for God's sake defend him from the cats and cads.' When Grey rose you could hear a pin drop. His biographer Keith Robbins tells us, 'White and silent he stared at the enemy and then spoke: "If arguments are not to be listened to from the Prime Minister there is not one of us who will attempt to take his place." He sat down to cheers and for the first and last time the Foreign Secretary was seen flushed and angry.'

Edward Grey held one of the two most important offices of state from 1905 to 1916, eleven years to the day; the longest consecutive period in office that any Foreign Secretary has ever served. The very fact that he held office for so long and over one of the most turbulent periods of our history, both domestically and internationally, speaks for itself. He was the most trusted and respected statesman on the European stage in the run-up to the First World War, and an irreplaceable member of Asquith's government. His overriding achievement was to take the country, parliament and the large majority of the cabinet united into war. What is more, thanks to Grey's diplomacy over the preceding decade, Britain entered the conflict with both the Empire and a powerful group of international allies on her side.

Grey once said that you had to be happy to write a book. If that is the case then surely, while married to his second wife Pamela Glenconner in the 1920s,

Grey was enjoying one of the most contented phases of an eventful life. Nobody was more deserving, for his distinguished career had been full of tragedy. His biographer, George Macaulay Trevelyan, wrote, 'It became part of Edward Grey's life that every person with whom he desired to make a home with for life was doomed to die and that every habitation in which he loved to dwell was burnt to the ground.' Needless to say this happiness was short-lived. *The Charm of Birds* was published in 1927 and Pamela died the following year.

The Charm of Birds became an immediate bestseller on publication, and established its author as a nature writer in the same class as W. H. Hudson, Gilbert White and Izaak Walton. To this day *The Charm of Birds* and *Fly-Fishing* remain the greatest books on their subjects. 'Grey wrote like a dream,' wrote the celebrated ornithologist James Fisher. Grey not only possessed an extensive knowledge of birds but was also capable of presenting the subject in an attractive and readily assimilated form to his readership. As a well-known public figure whose writing did much to popularise an interest in birds, he must claim much of the credit for the development of ornithology from amateur hobby into serious science.

Deep in his heart Grey felt more the countryman than the statesman. He loved fishing, birds, trees, gardens and the elements. In the same way he was a writer rather than an ornithologist, and certainly no 'twitcher' in the modern sense of the word. Thus *The Charm of Birds* describes the songs of everyday British birds – rarities were of no interest to him. It should not be forgotten, however, that although Grey delighted in the romance of birds, some of his observations on bird behaviour and migration nearly one hundred years ago display a knowledge somewhat more sophisticated than might have been expected from a country gentleman enjoying solace and recreation.

Grey's love of nature gave him the strength to carry out his public duties. His close friend and cabinet colleague Sidney Buxton wrote, 'Above all Edward Grey possessed the sense of country and all that it implied. This passion did much to keep his brain clear and his mind unclogged.' It is ironic that Grey's career at Westminster, by necessitating lengthy absences from the countryside, sharpened his appreciation for nature's mysteries and produced such a talented writer.

We can thank both Grey's wives, Dorothy Widdrington and Pamela Glenconner, for *The Charm of Birds*. Grey married Dorothy, an intelligent, shy and introspective woman who lived near the Grey family home at Fallodon in Northumberland, just after he came down from Oxford in 1885. They were devoted to each other and united in their common interests; it was Dorothy who ignited Grey's passion for birds.

He was devastated by her early death in a driving accident near Fallodon Hall in 1906.

While Grey was attending Winchester College he developed an enduring love of the river Itchen and the skills of dry-fly fishing. In 1890 he purchased a plot of land from his cousin Lord Northbrook at Itchen Abbas and built a small fishing cottage. Every weekend in the spring and early summer Edward and Dorothy would come down to their riverside refuge and fish for brown trout, read Wordsworth and listen to their beloved birds. They kept a diary of their visits to the cottage, which describes in charming detail the changing seasons, the bird song and other delightful encounters with nature. Grey privately published *The Cottage Book* in 1909, as a testament to the happiness they found together; it is a treasure-trove of happy memories on which Grey would draw thirty years later when writing *The Charm of Birds*.

Yet it was Pamela who we really have to thank. Like Dorothy she shared many of her husband's interests, notably books, poetry and birds. She had a strong and beneficial creative influence over a long period of his life, and it was she who encouraged Grey to sit down and write. Pamela's influence can be detected throughout *The Charm of Birds*. She was herself an accomplished writer, and two of my favourite passages, the description of the dawn chorus and of a goldfinch nesting amongst apple blossom, represent her work. Grey's brilliant impressions of the songs of the goldcrest, corn bunting and blackcap can be traced directly to Pamela's book, *Shepherd's Crowns*, published four years earlier than *The Charm of Birds*. Grey also wrote his autobiography, *Twenty-Five Years*, and *Fallodon Papers* when married to Pamela. Interestingly enough there is only one oblique reference to Dorothy in *The Charm of Birds*: 'A wren sprang into the air and singing in ecstasy as he flew, passed straight over me and over the cottage roof to some other place of bliss on the farther side: Like a blessing, said one who was with me.' When Grey died in 1933 his ashes were laid next to Dorothy's in the garden at Fallodon.

The Charm of Birds is a celebration of the joy and fulfilment that nature can bring to our lives, and is quite possibly the best book on birdsong ever written. Aside from its pleasing musical quality birdsong is a most effective marker for the changing seasons. Within this calendar there is always a sense of anticipation, an event to look forward to, a constant source of happiness. Every year, in the third week in March, I undertake a pilgrimage to Exbury Gardens beside the Beaulieu river. Here, looking across the Daffodil Meadow to Bucklers Hard, I listen for that harbinger of spring, the chiffchaff, amongst the thousands of azaleas and rhododendrons, which generate an exotic flavour under the canopy of the old forest. Later in the summer, when the leaves hang heavy on the trees, what the eye cannot see the ear can pick out. 'This is why the first hearing of a chiffchaff moves us each spring,' Grey writes in his chapter called 'The Return of the Warblers'. 'He is a symbol, a promise, an assurance of what is to come.'

Grey's crowning achievement in *The Charm of Birds* is to convey in the written word the songs of individual birds. 'There are two reasons to account for the difficulty we find in describing the songs of birds,' Pamela Grey wrote in *Shepherd's Crowns*. 'One is that those who listen intelligently to the bird songs hear them so differently and the second is that the birds themselves, individual birds of one species, in a certain degree, vary.' Grey's success lies in his ability to use an image to plant the individual song in form and sound in the memory. Hence with the goldcrest he writes, 'The song suggests to me a tiny stream trickling and rippling over a small pebbly channel and at the end going over a miniature cascade.' Again, with the nightjar, 'It is that class of stationary, soothing, continuous sounds such as the hum of a threshing machine, or the noise of the waves on the shore heard at a distance which dispose us to sit still and listen indefinitely.' Another effective tool Grey uses when describing birdsong is a comparison of individual bird nature with that of man. He finds the chaffinch's song both hearty and irritatingly persistent: 'If the chaffinch

were human one can imagine he would say cheerio.'
Likewise of the boisterous sparrow, 'It doesn't miss
much,' and of the fidgety, noisy sedge warbler, 'The
sedge warbler is the comic spirit amongst birds. The
eye-stripe gives it a jaunty look; its demeanour and
movements are very lively.'

What I find most moving about *The Charm of Birds*
is that it is so evocative of my own experiences. A
starling imitating a curlew, a mistle thrush singing
from a lofty perch in a December gale, meadow pipits
being flushed by pointers, yellowhammers singing
from hedgerows on a sultry late summer's day, goldfinches in a July ash tree or a green sandpiper rocketing
off from one of my ponds in early August signifying
the beginning of the autumn migration; all are familiar
from Grey's pages. Grey's final chapters on keeping
wildfowl led me to start my own collection at home
in the Derbyshire Dales. His story of Elizabeth the
pintail is quite heart-rending, yet it dramatically
conveys the romance of birds; that feeling of elation
and satisfaction when an unpinioned home-bred bird
returns to the fold after many months away in the
wild.

Grey was a well-rounded man, and unlike many of
his colleagues in the House had enjoyed the benefits
of a career in business. In 1898 he became director of
the celebrated North-Eastern Railway, whose 'Flying
Scotsman' passed close by Fallodon on the main line

to London. In 1904 he was elected Chairman at a salary of £2,000 a year, only to stand down on his appointment to Foreign Secretary the following year. In retirement, from 1916 to his death in 1933, he kept in touch with the political world through the House of Lords, where he often spoke on conservation issues. Grey joined the Royal Society for the Protection of Birds in 1893, becoming a Vice-President in 1909; ten years later he chaired the Committee to review the Wild Birds Protection Bill. He also played an important role in the early days of the National Trust, where a new post of Vice-President was specially created for him in 1924.

Grey's crowning glory in retirement was being made Chancellor of Oxford University the year after publication of *The Charm of Birds*. As an undergraduate he had been an academic failure, indeed had been rusticated from Balliol in 1884, but he returned to take a third in Jurisprudence. Aside from leaving us *The Charm of Birds*, his lasting memorial is the most important and prolific organisation for scientific field ornithology in Western Europe, the Edward Grey Institute at Oxford University. It is surely a fitting testimonial for a great Foreign Secretary and a passionate countryman.

Early Song

Bird life has many aspects, and each aspect has a peculiar attraction for us. The plumage of birds, infinite in diversity and beauty: their ways on land and water, and especially their ways in the air: their residence or migration: their mating, courtship, and care of their young: the eggs, so plain or so variously marked: the nests, so curiously made, differing so much in structure and in place chosen for them: and above all; the song of birds. Some mammals, reptiles, or insects make noises that are peculiar to the mating season; or that seem to express an emotion that is pleasant to them; but the song of birds, the set performance, variety, and musical quality, for instance of a nightingale or a song-thrush or a starling, surpass similar efforts in all other orders of life, excepting only that of mankind.

Let the song of birds, therefore, be considered first.

Most country people know the very common birds by name and by eye; it is remarkable that very few know them by ear. As a boy I was no exception. My earliest recollection of being called to notice the songs of birds is as follows: it must have been when I was nine years old, or less, otherwise I should have been at school and not at home at the time. It was a fine warm day, presumably late in May or early in June, for the trees were in leaf. The air was resounding with the singing of birds: my father was sitting with windows wide open at the writing table in the library; he called me to him and said, 'Do you hear all those little birds singing?' 'Yes,' I said. 'You wouldn't like to kill them, would you?' he asked; and I, somewhat reluctantly, said 'No,' because I knew this to be the answer expected or even required of me; but feeling in my inner self that if I had a weapon of precision, nothing wild and animate, not even little birds, would be safe. The propensity to sport had shown itself in me already by constant efforts to hit birds with a bow and arrow, a pursuit that had not been forbidden because it was at my age so futile; but perhaps it was this that prompted my father's question. Nevertheless though my father lived a country life and was fond of all sorts of country sport, of farming and of woods and fields, I do not remember that he had any individual knowledge of bird songs. From my father, and from the gardener and the gamekeeper with whom I consorted when I could, I learnt to know the common birds by appearance and by name: or rather, it should be said, some of the common birds, for none of the warblers, not even the ubiquitous willow-warbler, was included in this knowledge. The name 'blackcap' was indeed familiar to me and so was the bird that went by that name among the country people; for in hard weather it was frequently to be seen feeding on a rabbit carcase or some meaty morsel: it was in fact a marsh-tit. No one seemed interested in the songs of birds. My parents or grandparents would perhaps remark, 'How well the blackbirds and thrushes are singing,' or take some favourable notice of the fact that birds were singing, but it would be quite a general remark, and it is not probable that they knew the distinction between the song of a thrush and that of a blackbird, which they classed together. Thus I arrived at the age of manhood knowing only two songs of individual birds: one was the robin, whose tameness and persistence in singing when there is hardly another song to be heard force everyone to know his voice: the other was 'thrushes-and-black-birds' between which I could not distinguish, and which for the purpose of song represented to me one species. This state of ignorance is recalled not so much for the sake of personal recollection as because it is typical of ordinary country life. No one ever said to me, 'I heard the first willow-warbler today,' or, 'I wonder how many hundred times that chaffinch has repeated his song this morning'; and I grew up without identifying even such common songs as these.

It is song that is the most pleasing feature of bird life, but it is the last to arouse in most people any keen or intelligent attention. The reason is, no doubt, that birds offer so much that is attractive to sight, and the eye takes precedence of the ear in interesting us.

It will not be easy to give an orderly account of bird songs: perhaps the best method will be to take month by month in order, and thus trace the growth of song through the first half of the year; and to say as each species is named what it is that I have observed or felt about the song.

All birds cease singing for a long or a short time during the moult that follows the breeding season. Some time in the summer, therefore, their song may be said to end: the beginning is when song is resumed, and as some birds are heard again in the late summer or early autumn, I suppose that one of these months should strictly be taken as the first month of renewed song. I shall, however, begin with January, although some of the birds that sing in this month have begun to sing long before January. We are accustomed to the order of the months in the almanac, and any departure gives a feeling of discomfort. Is it not, for instance, an aggravation of the discomfort of income-tax returns that the financial year is made to begin on the 5th of April instead of on the 1st of January?

In January the mornings begin to lengthen. The evenings begin to do so about the middle of December, but the mornings get darker till the end of the year. It is not till January that the sun rises earlier, as well as sets later, every day. It is in the middle of this month that the greatest average cold of winter is reached and passed. Thus January may be said to be the month from which we may date the beginning both of longer and of warmer days; though the increase of warmth is so hesitating and slow for several weeks, that it may be considered technically rather than practically correct to notice it.

January, then, shall be described first, but the description will apply only to an average winter: exceptionally severe or exceptionally mild weather produces variations in bird life which must be allowed for.

The place in mind will be Fallodon, in the north-east part of Northumberland, on stiff clay soil, at no great altitude above the sea level, from which it is separated by some two miles of exposed land, now mostly grass. A high ridge of moor lies three miles to the west. Near the house are sheltering woods, and in the grounds are two ponds and plenty of shrubs: in short, a place attractive to birds, but with no unusual characteristics. What is heard of bird song here may be heard in any suitable place in the North of England. In an average January there will be some frost, and for a week, perhaps, a few inches of snow; but the ponds will be clear of ice for half the month, and there will be several days on which the thermometer in the shade will reach something between 40 and 50 degrees. It is on these days that the best singing will be heard.

First let the robin be noted. He has been singing since August, whenever the weather was not unduly discouraging, and he will go on singing till July. W. H. Hudson told me that the female as well as the male robin sings: this seemed probable, for in autumn each robin is alone in its territory. No robin will then tolerate a companion of its own or even of the other sex. Yet in each territory there seems to be song. The observations of Mr Burkitt with ringed birds, of which the sex had been ascertained and could be identified, has proved that female robins do sometimes sing like the males. I have, however, never heard the female sing after the birds have paired for the breeding season: of the pairs that I have had under observation only one bird has sung, and I conclude that this has been the male. Certainly only one bird has sung at a time and one has been silent, when they were together. If any one suggests that it is sometimes the male and sometimes the female that sings, I can only say that I think this is unlikely, but I must admit that robins are capable of anything.

Is there a difference between the quality of robin song in autumn and in spring? I think there is. In autumn the song has something thin and acid in its tone. 'The bitter note of the robin' was the comment of a friend, as we passed close to a bird singing in October. In spring the song seems more vigorous: it is worthwhile to stand close to a good robin and listen attentively: some notes of fine quality will be heard. In April, when thoughts are turned towards summer warblers, I have even heard one or two notes in a robin's song that prompt the exclamation 'blackcap!' In estimating the difference between spring and autumn songs allowance must be made for the human mood and expectation of the mind. In autumn, when:

> The warm sun is failing,
> The bleak wind is wailing,

when:

> The chill rain is falling,
> The nipped worm is crawling,

and the sun is getting lower and the days shorter, our own minds are attuned to a minor key, and we find it in the robin's song. On a warm April day, when sap is rising and we are full of anticipation, with ears a-tiptoe for the first note of a blackcap, we judge the robin's song differently. 'We used,' said a Conservative who was cutting my hair soon after the war, 'we used to think Mr Lloyd George everything that was bad. Now we admire him. Is it he or is it we that have changed?' And so I ask, listening to a robin in spring and comparing the impression remembered of the autumn, 'Is it the song or is it I that have changed?'

Be this as it may, the robin's song is worth attention: he sings more than any of our birds; he may be heard in every month in the year, even in July and August, if we listen for him: and, though he may not open the great chorus at dawn in May, he is the last to cease in the evening, outstaying even the thrush.

The wren shall come next. Of the wren, as of the robin, it may be said that in a not unfavourable year its song may be heard in every month, but not so certainly as that of the robin. It is pleasant to make a point of hearing a wren sing at any rate once even in the most silent month, but there are times when this is not accomplished without trouble and anxiety. In a fairly mild January, however, the hearing of a wren's song should be assured. The wren's song is a succession of rapid notes, forming a long musical sentence, that is repeated again and again at intervals. The full sentence is a long one, but the bird very often begins it and leaves off in the middle or even after the first few notes: a good example of what we were taught at school to call 'aposiopesis'; like the woman who, after speaking for a time at a public meeting, began a sentence with the words 'But still ...' then stopped and sat down. But when a wren is in good form he sings, as it was said the young Queen Victoria danced at a Court function in Paris, 'with decision, and right through to the end'.

To appreciate the song, however, the person of the wren, as well as its voice, must be taken into account. The song is a good loud one, but when considered in relation to the tiny body, it is positively mighty. 'Valiant,' 'resounding,' are epithets that I have applied when listening to a wren singing: and a little boy, whose mother had taught him to be familiar with the song, spoke, while doing lessons in an open-air parlour, of 'that shattering wren'. Great as the effort of the song seems to be, a wren at the height of the season will repeat it at short intervals for a long time without tiring.

There are individual wren songs that stand up like little peaks in memory.

Once, in days of youthful ignorance, a loud song proceeding from a thick cypress arrested my attention. It was long ago, in March 1884. I wondered what bird this was, and struck the branches with my stick. Out flew an unabashed wren, to perch elsewhere, and repeat the singing. The contrast between the size of the body and the strength of the song impressed itself on me, then and there, never to be forgotten.

There was another occasion, some years later. We had a cottage in the Itchen Valley, and had gone there early on a Saturday morning after a weary week in London; it was about 8 o'clock on a fine warm morning. I had just arrived, and stood in the doorway that opened on to the little lawn. Escaped from London at this season of the year, on such a day and in such a place, with the weekend prospect before me, I was indeed 'standing on the top of golden hours': in front, some ten yards away, was a poplar tree, and from it a wren sprang into the air, and, singing in an ecstasy as he flew, passed straight over me and over the cottage roof to some other place of bliss on the farther side: 'like a blessing,' said one who was with me.

Wordsworth in the 'Prelude' records an incident, differing in mood and setting, but similar in kind, in which the song of a single wren animated a ruined chapel. This was remembered, and added to that store of 'emotion recollected in tranquillity,' which he gives as a definition of poetry.

A third memory is of recent date. The incident occurred in the greenhouse, where a wren was in the habit of coming and going through open windows or ventilators. I heard the wren singing with even more than usual violence, perched somewhere among the plants. The cause was plain – another wren was singing outside, and there was a song combat. When two birds in neighbouring territories are singing in rivalry, it is the rule that they do not sing together: each in turn listens while the other sings; then the bird that has listened replies. So it was now. The greenhouse wren was used to seeing men about the plants, but besides this familiarity, it was so intensely occupied in listening to the song outside and then exerting itself to the utmost in reply, that it took no notice of my approach. I watched it for some time at a distance of not more than two or three feet, perhaps even less. The strophe and antistrophe went on: the attitude of my wren when listening was intent and still; when it replied the animation and vehemence were such that it seemed as if this little atom of life might be shattered by its own energy.

Not always, however, does the wren's song give this impression of force. On a bleak day in autumn, when chill wind is blowing, a wren's song will unexpectedly be heard, and at a distance will sound thin. Wordsworth describes this aspect of wren song:

> To the wind she sometimes gives
> A slender, unexpected strain.

It must not be inferred from the space given to it here that the wren's song is thought the best we have. It is a good song, clear, distinct, musical, and pleasant; it is elaborate rather than simple, and is well turned out. There are, however, other songs of higher quality, but the personality and song of the wren are so familiar and give so much entertainment that they cannot be passed over lightly.

Next, let us consider a songbird that attracts us not by smallness but by size – the mistle-thrush. He is the largest bird we have to whose performance the word 'song' in its narrower sense can be applied; but it would impoverish pleasure in birds so to restrict the thought of song. Every bird should be included that has what appear to be joy notes associated with courtship or some pleasant emotion, entirely distinct from the call or alarm notes. The curlew, the peewit, and the hooting of the brown owl are examples of this.

The mistle-thrush may be heard in mild winters before January, but I think of his song as generally beginning in that month: to be listened for then as a sign of reviving life in a new year. He is a bird that occupies a fixed station; that takes up a 'stance' for the express purpose of singing. This is one distinction that may be noted in the habits of songbirds: some sing from a fixed place, others sing as they go about their business of the day. Of the birds already mentioned the robin belongs to the first category, the wren, I think, mainly to the second, as do also the summer warblers.

The mistle-thrush mounts to the highest convenient stance he can find: he will resort to this same place day after day, like the song-thrush.

His song suggests to me a linked phrase, and here we come upon another possible classification of songbirds – those that, like the mistle-thrush and blackbird, express themselves in a linked phrase; repeated, after a pause, with slight, if any, variation: those whose song suggests rather a sentence than a phrase; this is repeated at intervals and is, as a rule, the same time after time. Of this the willow-warbler is a typical example. Thirdly, the birds whose song seems to be an improvisation of separate notes, not unlimited indeed in variety, but so indefinite in arrangement that we cannot be sure what notes are coming next. The song-thrush is the most complete and familiar example of this type of song.

The mistle-thrush is best appreciated in January and February. Not that he sings better then than later on;

indeed his song is more perfect in April, but it is very good in the two first months of the year, and it stands out clear in the then comparatively silent air. There are boldness and wildness as well as sweetness in the tone. It has not the rich and moving quality of the blackbird, and yet it stirs us. For on a windy day in January, when the blackbirds seek the shelter of laurels and thickets and have not a note of song in them, the mistle-thrush sings, aloft and conspicuous. There is, it has been well said, 'weather in his song'. Birds as a rule seem to dislike wind more than any other sort of weather, but the mistle-thrush is less discomfited by it than any other songbird. On a windy day early in the year the 'stormcock' will mount his tree, and there in full exposure proclaim by song that he is vigorous and glad. Every year he deserves to be honourably and gratefully saluted.[1]

The great tit must have his place among the song-birds of this month. His spring notes begin to be heard now. The rhythm of the notes suggests sawing, but they are evidently intended by the bird to be a song as much as that of any other bird that sings. I have known them to be mistaken early in the year for those of the chiff-chaff, before the latter bird has arrived.

The contribution of the great tit to the bird sounds

[1] Once in Rossshire in April I met with a mistle-thrush that besides the usual phrase shouted some notes that were quite unfamiliar: I saw and heard the bird in the same place on more than one day.

of this month is no mean one. The notes ring out loud, vigorous, and clear: to one who knows the ways of the great tit the sharpness of his notes suggests the sharpness of his beak. Among others of his own size he is a strong, bold bird, capable of tragedy, as the following story will show. There were traps kept in the garden for rats and other small nuisances. Some of these traps were cages so constructed that it was easy from outside to find the way in, but difficult from the inside to find the exit. Into one of these there had entered a dunnock[1] and a great tit. Presumably the dunnock had entered first, and the tit had come later, attracted by seeing the cage occupied. Whether the tit entered with fell design, or whether having entered he was roused by what Shakespeare calls 'vile opportunity,' we cannot tell, but the result is known. When in due course I visited the trap the dunnock was a pitiful sight: it lay dead; the skull was broken into and the brain had been eaten. The great tit alone was alive, a patent and thriving murderer.

---

1 I select this name from others given to this bird in order to avoid the use of the familiar but detestably inappropriate name, 'hedge-sparrow'. The dunnock or accentor is not more partial to hedges than some other sorts of birds. It does not resemble a sparrow in diet or disposition, and is not related to it. Emily Brontë knew the bird by this name, and also knew that it is frequently a foster-parent of a cuckoo. In *Wuthering Heights* Ellen Dean is asked what she knows of the history of Heathcliff. She replies, 'It's a cuckoo's, sir, ... and Hareton has been cast out like an unfledged dunnock.'

'What did you do with the horrible tit?'

'Madam, I set him free, not feeling competent to assess his moral responsibility in the matter.'

After all, do we not most of us follow the advice or instruction to 'kill and eat,' or eat what has been killed for us?

I have paid less separate attention to the notes of the other common tits, the blue, the coal, and the marsh-tit. There are certain notes of each that I hear in the earlier part of the year and look for as a sign of spring; the notes of the blue- or tom-tit are among my earliest recollections of the kitchen garden: for the sake of these the blue-tit is beloved. There is a happy huskiness in his voice, and his ways and appearance are very engaging. The willow-tit I have not yet distinguished from the marsh-tit, and with impaired sight I could not now discover it for myself. The crested tit I have only seen, and not heard. Its manners are very like those of the blue- tit, and suggest that the notes may resemble those of the bird to which it seems so nearly related. Long-tailed tits appear to be an exception in having no distinct notes for the breeding season. They utter two notes, which are familiar: one a tit-like call-note, but very high – almost as high and small as that of a gold-crest's, the other like a small soft rattle; but these notes they utter all through the year, and they appear to be company-keeping or call notes, and not akin to song.

One trick of the great tit must be mentioned before passing on: I have heard and watched at close quarters a great tit keep up for some time a perfect imitation of the 'pink-pink' of a chaffinch. The imitation was so perfect that, had I not been so close that the tit could be seen to be making the sound, I should have considered the performance by any bird but a chaffinch to be incredible. What the sex of this tit was I cannot say. I did not make a record of the time of year, but it was when the trees were bare and the tit was in full view on the lower branches of a beech tree.

Taken altogether, the notes of tits make a very animated contribution to the bird sounds of gardens and woods at the lively time of year.

The song-thrush shall come in at this point, though it is not so easy to decide his place as might be supposed. If it were the Avon or Itchen Valley that was being taken for the example of song, I should say that the thrush after his mid-summer silence begins to sing again in October, and continues to sing in mild weather till the next mid-July. On Sundays in November in the South of England, when I have been out for a walk with lunch in pocket, a thrush has, by his singing, decided the choice of a spot for luncheon. Indeed, in the South of England the thrush has only little more than two months in the year of complete abstinence from song. At Fallodon there is a great difference of habit: after the summer the thrushes leave the garden and woods. Very large numbers are to be found in turnips, collected there presumably by the attraction of some abundant supply of food. But when this is exhausted or the turnips are pulled, the thrushes do not return to the garden and woods about the house. When hard weather comes the lime trees close to the house become like a rookery of blackbirds waiting to swoop down on food put out for them. If there is a single thrush there it is remarkable. Yet thrushes in spring are as common as blackbirds about the house. Where are they in winter? Great numbers of thrushes are to be found on the links[1] in winter, and the fragments of snail shells to be seen round many a flat stone there explain the presence of the thrushes. I have not observed whether this autumn and winter withdrawal of thrushes is peculiar to Fallodon and places like it, separated from the coast and yet near enough to it for the thrushes to be influenced by the attraction of the links and the snails thereon. Nor can I say whether these thrushes on the links are the same birds that have left and will presently return to the garden; or whether they are more distant migrants. One thrush, which was so tame as to be distinct from others, was to be seen at the cottage in Hampshire during every month of the year

1 This is the rough ground by the sea. It has no necessary connection with golf, though golf courses, especially the ancient and famous, were made on the links.

except December and January; and as I did not see him in those months only because I did not visit the cottage, there is no reason to suppose that he went away at all. For three or four years he was there, which is sufficient proof that some thrushes move as little in the year as some robins or blackbirds.

At Fallodon it is an exception to hear a thrush sing in the autumn, and not till January do they return to the garden: sometimes they do not come till February, but as I have heard one sing as early as the 11th of January in a very mild winter, the thrush shall be considered as beginning his song here in that month.

The thrush has a variety of notes, but the order in which he gives them is improvised. We may listen to a thrush for a time without hearing the notes we most desire, for some of his notes are much less agreeable than others; a musical phrase resembling 'did-he-do-it?' may be repeated two or three times and then abandoned for some other notes. In fact, the manner of the thrush when singing gives an impression of selection and choice of the sound that he will make next. He sings perched in a tree, to which he has mounted for this purpose. There he will maintain his position and his song for some time, especially about dawn and sunset, preferably on the same tree day after day, pausing in his performance as if to select and choose his notes. Probably if birds were to be regarded as endeavouring to please us by song, the thrush should be put first among British birds. He does not rank in the very highest class for quality, but he certainly comes high in the second class. His is undoubtedly a major song, and owing to the number of thrushes, their persistent singing and the many months in which they are to be heard, we hear more of their song in the South of England than that of any other bird, except the robin. In song the thrush seems to be working very hard to please, and he succeeds. His song, too, can give a very pleasant impression of quiet contentment as well as of exultation.

Occasionally a thrush will introduce some freak sound and make it part of his song. Many years ago an attempt was made to keep white-faced whistling ducks in the collection of waterfowl at Fallodon. They are not hardy, but one of them survived for about two years, and being very tame, as is the manner of its kind, the whistling note with which it saluted everyone it saw became the most distinct and familiar sound in the garden. In January it died. In the following April we came home for Easter, and from high up in a silver fir by the pond came a perfect imitation of the call of the white-faced whistling duck. It was made by a thrush, but the bird did not continue the imitation after this spring, though it was often to be heard during that Easter holiday.

Another example was that of a thrush in the garden at Wilsford in the Avon Valley. For four seasons, at least, it sang continually during May and June on two notes; they were none of the usual notes of thrush song: they were as monotonous, but louder or more staccato than those of a chiff-chaff; and the persistence and monotony of them were wearisome. Nevertheless we listened for them every season in the same region of the garden. Last year (1925) my wife and I ascertained by close observation of the bird that he could, and sometimes did, sing the ordinary song of the thrush, so that his preference for loud monotony was due, not to incapacity, but to perversity. His freak song was not an imitation of any other that I know. So remarkable and well known did the sound become that the bird came to be spoken of in the family as 'Monotone'. We never heard him in the autumn or winter, but in spring the first hearing of 'Monotone' was noted, welcomed, and announced with as much satisfaction as the first news of a chiff-chaff or willow-warbler.

Two more birds that are certain January singers even in the North must be mentioned. The first is the starling. His song (for his very musical performance must be given that name) has been heard all through the autumn. When thrushes do not sing it is the most valuable and conspicuous event in bird music during the autumn and winter: every evening about sunset a starling, or a little party of them, sits on the top of a bare tree and gives a variety performance; some notes are their own, others are plagiarisms more or less close to the original; some are perfect imitations. The note that seems to me to be peculiarly the starling's own is a very clear boyish whistle; with this are all manner of other sounds – poultry noises, the chatter of sparrows, the cry of a peewit – one never knows what is coming next. Some of the notes are very pleasant, even beautiful, and are a delight to hear. The starling cannot attain to the quality of a blackbird, but he can whistle so near to it that more than once in February have I stopped and listened, thinking that I had heard all unawares the first blackbird, till some chatter or chuckling satisfied me that it was only part of the starling's infinite variety. Where curlews breed, the spring notes of the curlew are a very favourite imitation. Nobody but a curlew can make that wonderful sound; but this does not deter the starling from attempting it, and the resemblance of the imitation to the original is sufficient to make us thank him. The starling is like a gramophone among bird songs, and it has chosen some of the best of which to make records.

Last September (1925) one bird was missing from a tame covey of young partridges that I was feeding. From another part of the garden came the call of a partridge so perfect that I went hopefully in search.

On one or two other evenings I heard the same call frequently repeated, but there was no living partridge to be found, and it was no doubt the trick of a starling (there were some singing at the time), though I did not catch the bird in the act of deceiving me.

Close to the house at Fallodon, standing single on the lawn, is an old elm tree. It is too large for that part of the garden: it is failing and becoming more unsightly every year, for some of the branches at the top are dead. Yet the tree is spared because those same dead branches that seem to dishonour the tree do in fact gain distinction for it. In September and October, while the tree is still thick with leaves, these bare dead branches at the top are the favourite assembling place of a small party of starlings. There they sit every evening about sunset, and one or more birds discourse. It is worthwhile to sit and listen to them, not for the interesting variety alone, but also for the beauty of some of the sounds they make.

The dipper or water-ousel shall complete this chapter. He is the most certain January singer, for even the hardest weather does not silence him. When the woods are hushed and white with snow, and the burn is pinched by frost, so that only a narrow dark channel of running water shows between the ice and snow at the side of it, there on some stone in the burn the dipper will stand and sing. It is water rippling over a stony bed that he frequents; the soft luxuriance of a chalk stream has no attraction for him. His song seems part of the sound of the rippling water, from which he is never away. 'I hear thee where the waters run' may well be said of the dipper. His song is very sweet and lively; it has no marked beginning or close, but goes on indefinitely. It is as if 'beauty born of murmuring sound' had passed into the bird who was giving it back as song to the stream whence it had come. I reckon that there are two pairs of dippers each with its own length of the little burn at Fallodon; and where a burn is narrow and the banks upstanding, one can approach close to the sound and listen with pleasure and with admiration of the birds' hardihood. Of this hardihood I had experience in the first week of a certain memorable March in Sutherland. Blizzard followed blizzard; feet could make but slow progress through the snow; wheels could not travel except where passage had been cut by man through the drifts, on a small section of road, and even this was blocked again by fresh blizzards, that obliterated man's puny efforts. The frost was intense; the river was frozen from bank to bank, except where the swift current kept some open water at the head of pools. Wildlife was helpless: sheep had to be searched for and dug out of snowdrifts: grouse in trouble and despair flew in bewildered packs about the white hillsides. At a little height above the river my friend and I were slowly making our way on foot through the deep snow. From an unfrozen stream below there came up to us the sound of a dipper, singing its full song, undeterred by the conditions that were distressing all other life, unaffected by the cold, undismayed by the desolation. It was another moment when the song of a single bird penetrates to the affections and abides thereafter in the memory.

Chapter II

FEBRUARY AND MARCH

Increasing Song

Considerable as the space given to January has been, there is at least one notable bird voice that has not been included – the hooting of the brown owl, which is familiar in January; but fuller notice of this shall be reserved for the autumn.

It must not, however, be thought that January is a month of great song. For the sake of bringing some order into the writing, certain birds have been described that are to be heard in the first month of the year, but the description has applied to their full contribution of song when it is at its best in other months.

January is a month of slender song: it is the barest
month of the year. In early December there are still
some leaves and autumn colour on elms and oaks,
and the temperature in the first week of December is
on the average above that of the first week of March.[1]
Yet even in January new life is apparent. Aconites
and snowdrops are pushing through the ground.
Ribes buds are swelling, and if we crush one of these
and smell it and taste it and shut our eyes, we
are transported by association of taste and smell
to summer days, when in the luxuriance of the kitchen garden the fruit is thick on the blackcurrant
bushes.

In February there is little change of average temperature: by the 29th January the mean daily temperature has risen from 37·9 to 39·7, but on the 22nd
of February it is still, after some fluctuations, only
39·7. Nevertheless the uprising of life is not to be
stayed: though the air remains cold, the earth on its
round through space is daily exposing the northern
hemisphere more to the sun, and there is perceptible
warmth in the sunlight. The ground is bright with
aconites and snowdrops, violets can be picked on the
plants at the foot of the garden wall; there are catkins
on the hazel and small leaves on wild honeysuckle,
and green appears on bushes of the currant kind, that

1 Specific statements about weather are taken from statistics in *Whi-
taker's Almanack.*

in some past time were planted in the woods at Fallodon.

The two months of February and March shall be taken together; in this period most of our resident birds come into full song.

First let me mention two of them that may probably or possibly be heard in January, even at Fallodon.

The dunnock this year (1926) I did not hear till February; then its song was soon established. The dunnock is quiet in colour and in manner, and in its demeanour towards other birds it gives an impression of meekness. A friend to whom this remark was made replied, 'Yes: but then it relieves its feelings by laying that wonderful egg.' It relieves its feelings also in song. The song is quite adequate in loudness, and is pleasant, but there is little shape or feature by which to remember it. I found it a difficult song at first to distinguish, till I became familiar with the 'timbre'. It is, in fact, by the 'timbre' that in the end we get to recognise bird songs and distinguish one from another with greatest certainty. There are many distinctive characteristics of songs, which have little or no resemblance to each other; but as years go on I think it is by the difference in tone that we tell most easily one from another when hearing several singing together: just as one may recognise the presence of a friend in company by the tone of the voice, without hearing or attending to what is said.

The dunnock's song has spirit and uplift, and he often chooses a conspicuous position on the top of a shed or of the garden wall. Otherwise he is unobtrusive. Seclusion in the stack of peasticks, collected for future use in the kitchen garden, is a favourite habit of the dunnock. It is not a shy bird; it frequents back premises of houses and the gardens behind them, and is easy to watch; its habits suggest not so much fear of man as an inclination to apologise for its presence.

The tree-creeper I have heard in January, but I hardly expect its song then. It is a very sweet little wisp of sound. At first I confused it with that of the gold-crest, and found it difficult to keep the two songs distinct. The distinction is now so clear that it is made automatically and without effort, and I can hardly say that one song now suggests the other to me. I have read in some book that the song of the tree-creeper is rarely heard. This is not altogether true. In many Aprils, when fishing a salmon river in Sutherland, with spruce, oak and beech woods on one bank, the songs of tree-creepers, as well as of gold-crests, have been heard, repeated frequently and abundantly for many days together. But it is true to say that the tree-creeper is a most capricious singer. Even on a most favourable day in April it is not safe to say, 'Let us go out, and we shall hear a tree-creeper.' On the other hand, he will surprise us by uttering his song in some month early or late, when we do not expect it. In 1915 the Russian Army was having a terrible series of reverses: unbroken bad news came for a long period. One day came news of a distinct Russian success at one point in the line. Someone on hearing it remarked, 'You can never depend on the Russians not to do well.' So it may be said of the tree-creeper, 'You can never depend on him not to sing.'

He is very decidedly not a set singer, but desultory: that is to say, he does not sit in one place for the purpose of singing, but utters his song as he goes about the trunk of a tree searching the bark: the song is not a separate part of the day's business, but is incidental and subordinate to it. It is many years since my sight enabled me to observe birds by eye, except when very close to me, but my recollection is that the tree-creeper opens the beak very widely to sing. It is a very attractive bird; the slender bill suggests a humming-bird; the back is a rich arrangement of brown colours; the under parts are silvery white, and the body has a delicate outward curve from head to tail as it searches the tree trunks. It works up a tree and never appears head downwards. Thus, when it has done with one tree it flies to the low part of another and begins working up again. Has anyone ever seen a tree-creeper still and at rest? It does not perch on twigs: it is always busy on the trunk or on the stem of some big bough. It does not seem to go into holes[1] like woodpeckers. There are several Sequoia Sempervirens at Fallodon, and in the soft red bark of these are many recesses forming little seats. An occasional small dropping below the edge of some of these suggests that little birds make use of them; if so, it may well be that they are the sleeping or resting places of tree-creepers.

Next shall come two songs of such importance that the hearing of either is an event in the early part of the year. At Fallodon I used to note the 5th of February as a possible date for first hearing the chaffinch; this year I did not hear one till the 13th, but then several began at once. His song is robust and buoyant. Warde Fowler gives a very apt description of it in one of his books. He compares the manner of it to a bowler running with quick steps up to the wicket, and then with an overhand turn of the arm delivering the ball; and he notes that when the chaffinch first begins to sing it cannot for some days 'deliver the ball'; it gets to the wicket and stops. To those who know the song this illustration will surely commend itself. I have known people complain of the persistent iteration of the chaffinch's song, and I must admit that it does suggest a happiness that is a little trivial and commonplace. If the chaffinch were human one can imagine that he would say 'Cheerio!' as a greeting

1 Except when nesting.

to a friend. It is pleasant to play with these criticisms of a chaffinch: to do so, when one has a sure affection for it, does not really lessen one's feeling for the song, but endears it. The song is so persistent and abundant, that from February well on into June it is a commonplace in the bird chorus; and yet one chaffinch stands out in my memory as does a single dipper and a single wren. It was in the Whitsuntide recess, when for a few precious days late in May or early in June I had escaped from Parliament and from London, whose 'season' is then so miserably unseasonable. The days were fine and bright. On a stone coping of a little parapet, that went round the roof at Fallodon, at a corner that faced due south, a chaffinch used to take its stand, and from that eminence day after day it pelted me with song whenever I went on the lawn outside. This one bird became a feature of the holiday, an embodiment of happiness proclaimed from the house-top. Wordsworth, in memory of a day spent by 'a little unpretending rill,' says:

> The immortal spirit of one happy day
> Lingers beside that rill in vision clear,

and for me the immortal spirit of those happy Whitsuntide days still lingers in the song of the chaffinch.

Up to the last week of June the chaffinch continues in vigorous song; then it ceases. In September an occasional subdued and imperfect song may be heard, but it comes to nothing, and the bird cannot be counted as an autumn singer.

I once heard a hen chaffinch sing. It was in May or June, at the cottage in the Itchen Valley. The bird sang on more than one day, and was observed more than once through field glasses while singing. The song was not remarkable, but it was distinctly a succession of song notes. It was not the same as that of a male chaffinch. Field glasses did not show any signs of male plumage on this bird; it had apparently no mate, and the performance suggested that it was due to some physical change in the bird, analogous to that which occasionally causes male plumage in the females of some species, though in this case it was manifested in the voice and not in the feathers. The incident is unique in my experience.

There is a greater event to come now than the first song of the chaffinch. Let us imagine a perfect day near the end of February: a quiet day, the sun shining, the air mild; we get a few such days in every normal February. A lover of birds is walking in the bare woods, pleased with the various songs that he has already heard this year, listening especially to the loud song of dominant mistle-thrushes, fresh as the bright air, clear as the blue sky above; while little rills of robin song pour into his ears. Suddenly attention is arrested by something more rare in quality than the song of the mistle-thrush; he stops, listens, hears it again, and is assured of the authentic notes of a blackbird. I have told elsewhere[1] how the trained and sensitive ear of Theodore Roosevelt selected the song of the blackbird as the best of all the songs that he heard on a certain day in early June in England. It is not possible to explain why the blackbird's notes excel and why they mean so much to us. To me there is something in it that I can best describe as intimacy. The songs of other birds please or delight us, but that of the blackbird seems to make a direct appeal to us and stirs some inward emotion. It is one of five[2] bird sounds for which I have a particular affection. The song is a linked phrase, repeated again and again at intervals. As a rule the bird chooses a perch for the purpose of singing, but occasionally changes its place and sings while flying from one perch to another. It is a supreme moment when a blackbird, passing from one bush of flowering hawthorn to another, as if one spot could not contain its joy, utters its song on the wing in the ecstasy of mid-May.

There is a general type of song common to all blackbirds, but sometimes one individual bird develops a phrase peculiarly its own, and can be identified by

1 'Recreation,' an address to the Harvard Union, published here and in America and reprinted in *Fallodon Papers*.
2 The other birds in mind are the nightingale, the blackcap, the curlew, and the eider drake.

this in the same place day after day throughout the season of song.

Blackbirds have a common trick of ending their song with an inferior note, almost a squeak. John Morley in his *Recollections* describes a visit he made with a friend to Renan. We are told how the old man was roused to interest, and we are made to feel the vigour and magnificence of his talk. Morley and his friend had planned to go to the opera, but with the glow upon them of what they had seen and heard of Renan, they felt that the opera would be bathos, and they did not go to it. Then Morley adds as an additional reason for not going to the opera, that, besides, he had to pack. The squeak or 'scritch' at the end of a blackbird's song, coming after the beautiful and fine notes that precede it, is like that – a sudden drop from heights.

A short four months of song is all that a blackbird gives us in the year. Indeed, he is not established in song till March, and he ceases before the end of June. Then he goes into his moult and becomes an untidy and deplorable object. I have, however, heard a blackbird singing well in St James's Park in July, even late in the month, if my memory is correct. Why this should have been so it is not easy to guess. It may have been a bird, let out from a cage, that had not mated and had escaped the exertions of the breeding season, and thus retained its vigour and delayed the moult. I remember being rather resentful that a London park should continue to have the privilege of blackbird song for some weeks after the birds had become silent in the country; but I hope it gave a little compensation to people unable to leave town.

One last word about the song. Let anyone who wishes to measure its value listen to the great dawn chorus in May; that half-hour before sunrise, when like morning stars all the birds sing together. Listen attentively and consider how the song of the blackbird gives tone and spirit to the whole. A dozen or more different species of birds are taking part, but it is the notes of the blackbird that the chorus could least spare.

Some other birds that come into song in this period must have a place in this chapter. The yellow-hammer, our gayest bunting, begins his song earlier than all his common British relatives. The formula for his song, 'A little bit of bread and no *cheese*,' is well known. The yellow-hammer, like the chaffinch, for the first few days has difficulty in finishing the phrase. He will accomplish the first part of it, and then stop. In fact, for some days he may be said not to be sure about his 'cheese'. The yellow-hammer is a great frequenter of roadside hedges, on the top of which he will sit and sing, and is one of the prettiest and most familiar sights of country walks. In the last week of February this year I found myself on such a walk passing between two yellow-hammers, each singing perfectly in alternate rivalry.

The yellow-hammer's song is continued very late in the summer, even into August. It is not a song of power or melody; its merit is in quaintness and familiarity: it draws attention to the bird when he is perched conspicuous on the top of a hedge or whin-bush, and it is always worthwhile to observe through field glasses the uncommon yellow head and the exceedingly rich brown colours of the back, for the mature cock yellow-hammer is a very handsome bird.

Walking one day with two friends to see birds in the New Forest in May, we came upon a very choice sight of bird colours. We were among some whins on an open heath, and there, at no great distance on the bushes round us, was a yellow-hammer, a linnet and a stonechat, all mature cock birds in brilliant plumage. It was a fine chance of turning the field glasses from one bird to another and admiring the beauty of each.

The song of the bird now to be described is probably more familiar and distinct to everybody than any other. The skylark owes his fame to the manner of his singing; it is part of a conspicuous joy flight. The bird sings both ascending and descending. I have not myself timed individual larks, but I am told that two minutes is an unusually long time for one performance. The bird is as visible as the song is audible, and there is no possibility of mistaking the singer or confusing it with any other bird: it compels recognition and attention. It has inspired fine lines of poetry, and there can be hardly a poet who has avoided all reference to it. In youth I preferred Shelley's to Wordsworth's poem on the 'Skylark,' but in later years Wordsworth's 'A privacy of glorious light is thine' got a firmer grip and was more satisfying than all the similes, beautiful as they are, in Shelley's poem.

Ruskin, in *Modern Painters*, draws a distinction between 'Fancy' and 'Imagination'; the latter he exalts as incomparably the higher quality. He gives Shakespeare's 'Daffodils that come before the swallow dares, and takes the wind of March with beauty,' as one instance of Imagination; as an instance of Fancy he gives Milton's 'Pansy freaked with jet.' There can be no question which of these two expressions stirs us and endears the flower most. So is it with me in comparing Wordsworth's and Shelley's poems on the Skylark. Shelley delights with the beauty of his poem, Wordsworth stirs our feeling for the bird.

I came across a small volume of verse written by a young airman in the war. There was no evidence that he knew Wordsworth's poem on the Skylark, but one of the experiences that he described as most pleasing or glorious was the sensation of being high up alone in the sunlight. When Wordsworth wrote 'A privacy

of glorious light is thine,' his imagination had pene-
trated to what man would feel in the skylark's place.
Without giving the bird human attributes, he had
linked its flight and song to human feeling. This is an
achievement in poetry that 'fancy', however beautiful,
cannot accomplish.

The skylark becomes an essential feature of country
life. I was walking from one plantation to another
with an old woodman: it was a fine April day: we
were crossing grass fields and skylarks were singing:
as bird after bird rose about us the old man said
aloud, but to himself rather than to me, 'Them
lav'rocks mounts and sings.' They were part of his
life. He was an intelligent man, but self-contained;
rough in manner with others, aloof and unpopular.
He had never seen London, and I arranged for him
to spend a week there. We went on the top of an
omnibus from Piccadilly to the City. 'Eh! what a
throng!' he kept repeating, as he looked down on
crowded streets and pavements; and finally, 'It's fair
like bees swarming.' He was interested in what he saw
in London, and enjoyed his week there, but after his
return home, when we were walking alongside an old
avenue, he remarked, 'I couldn't bear to live in a city
where I couldn't lift up my eyes and see the trees
standing one behind another.' If he had been told of
the city dweller who after a day or two of the country
fled from it because he could not stand the 'tingling

silence,' it would have produced nothing but the blank stare of inability to understand: so, too, the lover of the town can never understand the sense of depression, exile and exasperation that the country man feels when brought to live in a great city.

I have never lived in the company of woodlarks, and my acquaintance with them is confined to one or two expeditions, made to places where woodlarks were known to be, for the purpose of hearing their song. They are therefore to me like celebrities to whom one has once or twice paid a visit of ceremony, and I cannot speak of them with intimacy. As I saw the bird it sang on the wing, and the flight was less clearly a joy-flight than that of the skylark. The bird did not soar; it flew as if the flight might have some other object, such as change of place, combined with that of song; but song was evidently part of the object, though the bird also sang when perched on a tree. There were notes of finer quality than any that the skylark has: the shortness of the tail recalled the appearance of a bat in flight. The quality and sweetness of the notes and the manners of the bird were very pleasing, and I regret that it has not been my good fortune to live in company with woodlarks. The birds seem to thrive easily where there are trees and open ground, such as heath, and why with such abundance of apparently suitable country the woodlark should be so local is a tiresome mystery.

The meadow pipit is a bird that, being gifted with only a small song, displays it to the best advantage; it ascends to no great height – perhaps twenty feet or so – and then descends like a little parachute, singing as it comes down. Here again the song is evidently part of a joy flight, and when one is salmon-fishing in early spring in moorland country, meadow-pipits make a minute but perceptible contribution to the happiness of the day. They are very common in heather country, and though so small and, except when in song flight, so insignificant in their ways, they evidently have a strong scent. To the nose of a pointer or setter a moor must seem pervaded with the smell of meadow-pipits, and when grouse are scarce a dog will vary the monotony of finding no grouse by pointing a meadow-pipit, or 'tit-lark' as it is often called. The scene is only too well known to everyone who shoots grouse over dogs. The pointer becomes as rigid and earnest as if a covey of grouse were in front; the guns, if there are two, draw together and advance one on each side of the dog, which, encouraged by the keeper, moves forward with intense caution. At length a tit-lark flits unconcernedly out of the heather, the dog relaxes and wags its tail in a deprecating manner, as if asking us to excuse the joke since it is such a small one; and then, as if doubtful how the joke will be taken, starts off again in quest of the scent of grouse. Thus in one way or another the little meadow-pipit mixes itself with memories of Highland sport.

Some account of the smallest of all British birds shall conclude this chapter. It is only when we know the song of the goldcrest that we realise how common the bird is. It likes fir woods, but is not restricted to them; a fir here and there among deciduous trees contents it. One great silver fir in the garden at Fallodon, one cedar on the lawn at Wilsford, is each a whole world to at least one pair of goldcrests. Its voice, as we should expect, is very high-pitched; the little call-notes are like needle-points of sound. The song has little volume, but on a still day can be heard from some distance. It suggests to me a tiny stream trickling and rippling over a small pebbly channel, and at the end going over a miniature cascade. One hesitates to offer such an image of song, or indeed any image of song; some chance suggests one to the mind, and gradually it is so associated with the sound that to oneself it becomes inseparable from it, however fanciful it may have seemed at first: to anyone else it may seem so far-fetched as to be inapplicable. It is, however, worthwhile for those who attend to bird songs to encourage the image that a song may suggest. It becomes pleasantly associated with the sound, and may help to distinguish it. Probably it was this image of the song of the goldcrest that helped me to disentangle it so completely from the song of the tree-creeper.

The goldcrest is not an easy bird to observe, but this is because of its incessant activity; not because of shyness. It is not a shy bird, but this seems due, not so much to tameness as to indifference: the indifference that small insects show towards large things such as human beings. Once when I was sitting among whin-bushes in the New Forest a goldcrest came so close to my face that it suggested the need of reading-spectacles to peruse it.

The Return of the Warblers

Let it be supposed that the two preceding chapters have brought us to the March Equinox. Enough has been said to show that the amount of song to be heard now is considerable; and yet there are other bird sounds to be heard in this period which are of great importance throughout the spring, and have not been mentioned. The cooing of wood-pigeons, the spring notes of curlews and peewits, the performance of snipe, are examples of what has been omitted. These are manifestations of the spirit of song, but they can only be comprehended in the term 'song' by giving the word a wider definition than is convenient. The fuller notice of them shall therefore be kept for a later chapter.

Although on favourable days in March the volume of song is considerable, it must not be inferred that even March is a great month of song. George Meredith has written somewhere that February blew south-west for the pairing of the birds: March can blow north-east for the silencing of the birds. There are many days in March that might be regarded as an embodiment of what Goethe calls 'the Spirit that denies': days that wreck with wind and thrust life back with cold. In one respect February and March are less favourable to birds than other months in the year. Birds need moisture and February and March are, on the average, two of the least wet months.[1] The term 'February fill-dyke' is often quoted, and it is accurate though misleading. It is accurate because the springs of water are high and the earth wet from autumn and winter rains and melting snow, and dykes are therefore full; but it is misleading if taken to mean that February is a wet month. The rising of the sap and the courtship of birds have therefore to press on against many days of cold, dry wind; but in March, even more than in February, a few days may be expected that are bright and still, or mild and moist. On these days, made precious by contrast with the others, the outburst of

---

[1] Rainfall varies in different parts of the British Isles, and statements as to the dryness or wetness of each month that are true of one district may not apply to another. April on the whole may be said to be the driest month of all, and February, at any rate in some places, comes next to it. It is interesting to note that these two dry months are the two which in popular speech are particularly associated with wetness – February 'fill-dyke' and April showers.

bird song is a manifestation of the general uprising of life, and proves how invincible is the impulse towards growth and reproduction, and how all things are confident of the ultimate victory. Summer is coming up from the south, and even in March there arrive in England some birds that took refuge from our winter in the warmth of Africa. The Thick-knee comes back to us, wheatears begin to flit about the Hampshire and other South Downs, as familiarly as if they had been there all the winter. Sand-martins, the advance birds of the swallow kind, may be seen in a normal year before the end of March; and the chiff-chaff should be heard. Here, be it noted, my recollections are transferred from north to south, and for some weeks onward the places specially kept in mind will be the Itchen Valley with the country surrounding Itchen Abbas and Avington; and the Avon Valley and the country about Wilsford, not far from Stonehenge.

To those who mark the progress of the year by the song of birds, the first hearing of the chiff-chaff is the beginning of a new stage. Hitherto we have noted the coming into song of resident birds; in the chiff-chaff we hear a bird proclaiming not only that he is singing, but that he has arrived. He has accomplished, since we last heard him, two long journeys, one away from us in the autumn, and now the journey of return. Alone of all the warblers, the chiff-chaff has given us the right to expect him in March; he is the forerunner of the rush of songbirds that is on its way to us and will arrive in April, and thereafter enrich our woods, meadows and gardens with still further variety and quality of song. This is why the first hearing of a chiff-chaff moves us so each spring. He is a symbol, a promise, an assurance of what is to come. In himself the chiff-chaff is a very individual and peculiar little bird. I will not attempt to define the word 'warble' or 'warbler'. The term has become so inseparably attached to certain summer birds that there is no choice but to continue the use of it; though if it is to be used at all, there is no justification for its being restricted to the class of birds that are habitually called 'warblers'. There is, however, no conceivable utmost stretch of definition by which the term 'warble' can be made applicable to the sound that the chiff-chaff makes. On the other hand, if anything is to be called 'warbling,' the song of the willow-warbler must certainly be put in this category: and the chiff-chaff is so nearly allied to the willow-warbler that they must be thought of as members of one family. In appearance, habits, food, habitat and manner of nest the two birds have very close resemblance to each other; so close as to make the difference of song remarkable. By the season and manner of utterance the chiff-chaff gives us clearly to understand that he intends his notes to be a song, and as such I, at any rate, accept it from him.

Ill-disposed persons may say that it is nothing more

than chirping: against this assertion I should protest. There is a spirit in the two notes of the chiff-chaff that suggests the same motive as song, and there is something more than the mere reiteration of two notes. To one who listens attentively there is the hint of a pattern in the variation of the notes. The sound also suggests industry, as of the passage of a shuttle to and fro. Certainly the chiff-chaff is a very persistent and industrious performer. There is not, as a rule, more than one pair in the garden at Wilsford, but the notes are so frequently uttered and for such long periods of the day, that they are one of the most familiar sounds of the garden: if one did not observe that the sound came always from the same region, the impression would be that the garden was full of chiff-chaffs. Like other songbirds, the chiff-chaff becomes comparatively silent when strenuously engaged in feeding the young; but some time in the latter part of June he will for some days 'sing' throughout the day as if he had nothing else to do. The notes then have not quite the vigour of April and May, but they are even more frequently and continuously repeated. Then comes the moult, and the bird falls silent till September, when energy is restored and expresses itself in a subdued repetition of the 'song' – a sort of quiet farewell before the chiff-chaff leaves us on its long journey southwards.

The chiff-chaff has, in fact, named itself, for the

name is suggested by the sound of its notes. The bird has therefore the good fortune to be well named. Its nearest relation, which arrives early in April, is unfortunate in the matter of its name. It is usually spoken of as the 'willow-wren.' The name is not so offensive and vulgar as the name 'hedge-sparrow' is when applied to the dunnock, but it is inappropriate. The bird is not a wren; this name should be kept for the common wren, a bird so distinct and individual among British birds that its title should be kept for it alone and not shared by any other species; though perhaps a concession to ordinary usage may be made in favour of the gold-crest, which is often called the golden-crested wren. Nor is the so-called 'willow-wren' more partial to willows than other birds that frequent trees and bushes. In places where I have observed willow-wrens to be particularly abundant there are no willows, nor the moist ground that willows desire. It would, however, be futile to invent an altogether new name for this bird: it has already the alternative name of willow-warbler, and I propose to use this name, as being the less inaccurate of the two. Of all our summer warblers this seems to me to be the most widely distributed. I have never been in any part of England where it is not common; in the woods about Fallodon it is so abundant that the song forced itself upon my notice before I had begun to take any account of small birds: all day and every day in May and early June, when I was in the woods, the song of one willow-warbler after another was in my ears: it was impossible to ignore it. Not knowing from what bird it proceeded, I called it 'the everlasting bird,' because the songs seemed never to cease. In the South of England one expects to hear it in the first week of April. The song is particularly pleasant as well as frequent. It is a succession of slender and delicate notes, forming a completed sentence, which is repeated again and again at short intervals. The bird is a desultory singer, uttering its song as it flits about the bushes, searching the leaves for insect food. The notes have a very endearing quality of their own. They suggest something plaintive – as if the bird were pleading. 'A cadence soft as summer rain' has occurred to me when listening to the song, which is peculiarly touching. It is entirely without any note of bravado, exultation or challenge, such as is suggested by many other songs. To all who find pleasure in birds, the arrival and first hearing of the willow-warbler each spring is a moving incident. In the summer moult the willow-warbler becomes silent, but in September it sings for a little, infrequently and rather faintly. The resumed song has in it something meditative and reminiscent. This, at any rate, is the mood it suggests to us: then unnoticed, the willow-warbler quietly slips away on its journey to another continent, to winter in Africa.

A bird to be thought of with the chiff-chaff and the willow-warbler is the wood-warbler. It differs from these two species more than they do from each other, but there is considerable resemblance. The wood-warbler (for the reason given already I prefer this title to 'wood-wren') is well named. It is a bird of full-grown woods. It does not frequent gardens and shrubberies, as the chiff-chaff and willow-warbler do: it lives in big trees, especially beech and oak: so indifferent is it to bushes that it seems almost to prefer woods, where the ground is bare, as is so often the case under beech trees.

The wood-warbler is brighter in colour than the willow-warbler: it looks a stronger bird, and the length of the wings gives the impression of a shortness of tail, that causes the bird to look less slender and more robust.

The song is very remarkable: the bird has in fact two songs, so distinct and unlike that nothing but clear and close view can convince one that the different sounds are made by the same bird. Fortunately it is easy to watch it; for though it is often in the upper part of a big tree, it also descends to lower branches, and there, within a few feet of human eyes, it will continue its business of feeding and singing. So occupied is the wood-warbler in these pursuits, so apparently confident in the security of its own joy and innocence, that it seems not to mind being watched.

The open branches of big trees do not give the
exasperating concealment with which bushes baffle us
so often when we are trying to observe other little
birds. The time to watch and listen to the wood-
warbler is when the beech leaves are fresh and tender
on the boughs early in May: the soft green and yellow
colours of the bird are in tone with the foliage,
and its ways and movements and general happiness
animate the beauty of young beech leaves: wonderful
and perfect beyond description as this beauty is, the
presence of a wood-warbler can still add to it. The
song that is most frequent is the shivering or sibilant
sound, as it is called in books. To appreciate it one
must watch the bird singing, and thus get the impression of delight that is in it. When this has been
watched and remembered, the song will always suggest
a little ecstasy, whether the bird is seen or not.

The other form of song is one clear and very
plangent note, repeated in gentle succession as often
as nine or ten times. The bird no doubt expresses the
same feelings by this as by the other part of its song,
but the impression made on a human listener by these
plaintive notes is one of intense sadness: the tone is
pathetic; there are tears in the voice. Sometimes a
wood-warbler will give these notes at no long intervals,
though never so frequently as the shivering notes; at
other times we may listen to these commoner notes
repeated again and again, at very short intervals, and

the bird will withhold the plaintive notes altogether. When this is so, we do not get a complete impression of the wood-warbler, for it is the contrast between the two songs that is characteristic of the bird, and indeed remarkable among all bird songs.

Warde Fowler in one of his books tells how he was puzzled when first making acquaintance with the wood-warbler. He thought he must be in the presence not of a single bird, but of two birds of different species. The passage was familiar to me before I had heard a wood-warbler, and when I did hear one for the first time I became aware that I was going through precisely the experience that Warde Fowler had described: thus to me the discrepancy between the two sets of notes was not a mystery, but a revelation. I have noticed the wood-warbler to be very abundant on the only two occasions when I have been in the New Forest in late spring, once early in June and once in the latter part of May. It seemed as if I passed, for two or three miles at a time in the heart of the forest, continuously from the song of one wood-warbler to another. At Fallodon there are several pairs in the woods near the house, but the earliest bird is not heard there as a rule till the beginning of May, three weeks later than the willow-warbler.

Two warblers of high rank in song must be considered together – the blackcap and the garden-warbler. There is close resemblance between them in habits, voice and nests: so closely allied are they that one pair seems jealous of the presence of another. Adjoining the cottage in Hampshire was a chalk-pit, overgrown with blackthorn, bramble, wild-rose, and much elder; there were also a few oak, ash, and maple trees. For all the thirty-three years that I knew the chalk-pit intimately, one pair of blackcaps nested there every spring. In the later years a garden-warbler was to be heard singing there early in May, but after some days he would be heard no more, and the song of the blackcap continued alone. My interpretation was that a pair of garden-warblers, attracted by the aptness of the place for their needs, endeavoured to establish themselves in it: the blackcaps, who had been in previous possession, regarded the garden-warblers as rivals and prevented them from settling in the chalk-pit. Other warblers nested there: one pair of willow-warblers every season, a pair of sedge-warblers generally, a pair of nightingales, and a pair of each species of whitethroat sometimes, but never more than one pair of the same species. The inference is that one pair of warblers will tolerate another of quite different species in the same territory, but the presence of a pair of blackcaps and the extrusion of the garden-warblers suggest that these two species were too nearly related for one pair of either kind to allow the other to inhabit the same territory. I have not observed the same intolerance between chiff-chaff and willow-warbler, though these kinds resemble each other even more closely in appearance than do the blackcap and garden-warbler. The two latter birds, on the other hand, have a resemblance in song that is rare, if not unique, as far as my knowledge goes, among British warblers. The conclusion is that it is resemblance of song rather than of habits or appearance that provokes animosity between birds of different species.

In appearance blackcaps are very distinct from garden-warblers: the size and shape are alike, but the blackcap is an exception to the rule among our warblers that both sexes should have the same plumage. The prevailing colour of each sex is a soft grey, but the male has a black cap, the female has one of rich brown on the top of the head. The general appearance of both is of elegance and good taste. Garden-warblers have the quiet greens and yellow colours of the willow-warbler – they are, indeed, like larger willow-warblers without an eye-stripe, and the sexes are alike in colour.

For perfection or moving quality of voice I should place the blackcap with the blackbird and the nightingale in the first class of British songbirds. His song is loud, exceedingly sweet, but also spirited: it is not very long, but is frequently repeated: there is not great variety, but the thing done is absolutely perfect. There is not a note that fails to please or to be a success. The tone does not stir us so inwardly as that of the blackbird, but it is sheer delight to listen to it. Of the blackcap, indeed, it has been said that, like the gipsy before the castle gate, 'he sang so very completely'.

The garden-warbler's song is very good: in one respect it surpasses that of the blackcap; it is more sustained; but the bird never seems absolutely to clear the throat and let out the sound so pure and free as the blackcap does. To my ear the opening notes of the blackcap's song and those of the garden-warbler are so alike that I hear them with a doubt of which bird I am listening to; but the garden-warbler goes on and on for a longer time and yet never seems to liberate its voice upon the air so completely as the blackcap does. In other words, a garden-warbler's song seems always on the point of an achievement, to which only the blackcap attains.

Having made this critical comparison between these birds, let me end as I began, by putting them together. They are rather larger than any of our warblers except the nightingale, and with this same exception they are greater in song than the others. I have never found either so abundant as the willow-warbler is in some places, but they are very widely distributed; and in all country places where I have lived in England there have been a few pairs every season in the neighbourhood; and though the two birds may not like each other, those who have an ear for bird songs are grateful to them both.

A number of other birds arrive in April that add to the variety of life and to the animation of English country, but are of minor importance in song. Two that are especially familiar to every dry-fly fisherman in chalk-stream valleys shall be noticed first – the sedge-warbler and the reed-warbler; though very few of the latter arrive before May.

It is impossible to write of the sedge-warbler without using epithets or expressions that apply to mankind rather than to a bird. When such expressions are used here or elsewhere, they are intended, not as literal descriptions of the bird's nature and character, but to give the impression that the bird's appearance and ways produce upon a human observer. The sedge-warbler is like a comic spirit among birds. The eye-stripe gives a jaunty look; its demeanour and movements are very lively. The natural song is apparently akin to that of the reed-warbler, but it is harsh in tone, and the bird interpolates various imitations of notes of other species. Warde Fowler, in a book already quoted, describes how he saw and heard a sedge-warbler imitate, as if in mockery, the fussy chuckle of a blackbird scared by a false alarm and flying off in unreasonable perturbation. The bird will often flit out almost under the angler's foot from some thick growth on the edge of the stream, as if its nest were surely there, when as likely as not the nest is in the hedge outside the water-meadow. Sometimes it seems to frequent the reeds, as if it made common cause with reed-warblers; and yet we come upon it in bushes on higher ground in dry places not adjoining water. It is as if the bird wishes to show us that it can be indifferent to the neighbourhood of water, which we have thought indispensable to it. It is lively and noisy all day, but also sings at night. If one sleeps out of doors, various birds, especially the dunnock, may be heard to utter an occasional snatch of song; but with the exception of the nightingale and grasshopper-warbler, the only one of our songbirds that I have heard sing frequently and even continuously at night is the sedge-warbler. The song lacks melody, but the bird is a pleasant and animating presence.

The reed-warbler's name is so literally descriptive of the bird as to be unimaginative and almost dull. It lives entirely in reed beds; it populates large tracts of reeds, such as are found in the Norfolk Broads, but wherever a rood or so of reeds grow we may expect to find a pair or two of these birds. Away from reeds I have never found it; and they must be the common reeds with long thin stems; sedge or other kindred growths will not serve its purposes. It is quiet and soft in colouring, and its song is a monotonous warbling, less varied but more melodious than that of the sedge-warbler, and pleasant to listen to. It sings continuously clinging to the stems of the reeds, among which it is invisible, except at a very short distance.

A moderate disturbance will start reed-warblers and also sedge-warblers singing. A friend and I were standing on a plank foot-bridge that led from one meadow to another across the Itchen; one end of the bridge passed through a belt of reeds. My friend was not very familiar with the reed-warbler's song and wished to hear it. A bird was singing in the reeds at a distance of some two or three yards, where we could both listen to it and watch it singing. Presently it ceased, but did not move.

'Would you like to hear more of it?' I asked.

'Yes,' replied my friend. I picked up some small missile and threw it into the reeds in the direction of the bird, which at once broke into song again. My friend was rather shocked, and to this day affirms that I nearly hit and killed the bird.

Reed beds have a delicate beauty of their own: especially is this to be noted on a sunny day in February or March. There is no young green in the reed bed yet, but last year's stems are cream-coloured; the dark feathery heads look silvery in the sunlight and nod like plumes as the wind agitates the innumerable reeds. The warblers have not come, but this is the time when reed beds have a peculiarly delicate and graceful beauty. Imagine such a day on the Norfolk Broads, where the spaces of open water between the cream-coloured reed beds are blue with the reflection of the sky.

As the new reeds grow up green in May the reed-warblers come and make their presence known. The time to listen to them is on a fine day in June, when there is just enough breeze to make a slight rustling in the tall reeds that blends with the continuous singing of the birds. Then we know the world in which reed-warblers live, and we feel the spirit of it.

The two whitethroats, the common and the lesser, arrive in April. I do not see much difference in size between them, but the common whitethroat is a little brighter in colour than the other: it is also more common, more conspicuous and lively in its habits, and altogether has a little more of everything noticeable than the lesser whitethroat. Its song is fussy, as if the bird were always in a hurry or slightly provoked. Sometimes the tones and manner suggest scolding. The bird is fond of roadside hedges which have thick undergrowth, and so thrusts itself upon our notice; but it also frequents clumps and woodland, especially where there are patches of bramble. In spite of what is said above about the bird and its song, the prevailing impression it gives is that of excitement and happiness, and its animation and vitality are a pleasant feature in the places that it chooses to inhabit.

The lesser whitethroat, though so like the other in appearance, is different in its habits. It is retiring and unobtrusive. I have not noticed it in roadside hedges but in quiet places, such as the thicket of a disused chalk-pit: and it seems to like large trees, to which the commoner bird, though not averse, seems indifferent. It needs bushes for a nesting place, but does not require a growth of nettles or other coarse herbage as the common whitethroat does. Its song is to me associated with warm days in June or even July: it is a monotonous repetition of one note, and suggests the syllable 'sip' repeated several times; then after a pause repeated in the same way. Altogether it is a curious contrast to the other bird in its comparative lack of animation and its quietness.

I have heard the lesser whitethroat utter notes like the song of the common whitethroat, and should have passed it by unless I had also heard the other song, but its characteristic song to me, founded upon observation of a pair that used to nest close to the Hampshire cottage, is the monotonous repetition on hot summer days described above. My observations with the lesser whitethroat are mainly in southern counties. I have, however, heard it more than once at Fallodon, where the other whitethroat is as common as anywhere else.

There are other arrivals in April, noticeably the corn-crake and the cuckoo, but this chapter had best be kept for birds that are, in the usual acceptance of the term, songbirds. Of these there are four others yet to be noticed.

The tree-pipit has a more considerable song than

the meadow-pipit, and as the name implies, it is a bird of the trees. From the top of a tree it springs up into the air and descends like a parachute, singing as it comes down to the perch from which it sprung or to another close by. The song is loud, and ends with notes that are very emphatic and determined. Sometimes the bird just sits and sings without leaving its perch at all. Of late years this otiose habit of the tree-pipit seems to have increased. The impression is probably due to accidents of my own personal observation: but the habit is one to be regretted, for the song when part of the little joy-flight, with its beautiful descent in air, is a very distinguished performance in bird song. Indeed, I resent being given the song without the display of flight, to which lovers of tree-pipits feel that they are entitled.

There is one bird classed as a warbler, but so distinct and unlike the others that it is difficult to write of it as a warbler. It comes with the rest in April, and is called the grasshopper-warbler. The sound it makes resembles the whispering noise of a grasshopper, but is more robust and louder: it is also like the noise of a small soft-running reel. In manner, delivery, motive and intention this sound is evidently a song. It ceases therefore after the breeding season, but while it is being uttered the whole attention and energy of the bird are given to it. The sound is made continuously, without apparent drawing of breath, and is kept up for some time. Willow-warblers and wood-warblers may sing intermittently as they flit among the leaves, but when the grasshopper-warbler sets himself to sing he can do nothing else. For this purpose he often chooses some dwarf willow bush in the rough ground that he frequents. There he will sit and 'reel,' turning his head occasionally from side to side, a motion which has the effect of making the sound appear now more now less distant to the listener, though the bird is stationary. As the summer advances and nights get warm, the grasshopper-warbler becomes a night singer. At Wilsford there is some rough marshy ground at the edge of the garden near the river. Here in 1922 a grasshopper-warbler sang on a single willow bush, and could be heard far into the night. The bird was not shy when singing, and in daylight could be watched only a very few yards away, so absorbed was it in its own performance. In one mile of the Itchen Valley that had much rough tussocky ground, too rough and coarse to be mown, there used always to be two, and sometimes three, pairs of grasshopper-warblers; and just when the evensong of birds had ceased in the warm dusk of June and July evenings, the grasshopper-warblers would begin to sing. Thus to me the song became associated with failing light and the end of a day's fishing. The territory of each bird became familiar to me, the presence of each was greeted every year and noted evening after evening on the way home in the quiet twilight: my waders, brushing through the lush, soft growth on the river bank, made a sound not out of keeping with that of the bird. Apart from the act of singing, the grasshopper-warbler is not seen: its small dark form is as unobtrusive in its ways as a mouse in the thick rough herbage, where the bird nests. The sound it makes suggests dryness, as if there were no moisture on the palate; the bird endears itself not by melody, but by the unusual and quaint character of its performance; its manner is very quiet, but the length of time for which the song is sustained gives an impression that the bird takes exceeding pleasure in it.

Some notice of two more birds that come to us in April shall conclude this chapter. The redstart is not a very important singer, but is sufficiently so for its arrival to be listened for every year and for the song to be picked out by ear and attended to as we walk about the woods. For some reason the bird does not seem to care for the chalk-stream valleys: neither about the cottage on the Itchen nor at Wilsford in the Avon Valley have I heard it. At Fallodon there are three or four pairs every season. I called a friend's attention to it there this year: he did not know the song, and after listening for a while said that the first part of the song reminded him of the chaffinch. At that moment a chaffinch sang close to us, and we listened to the two birds: the contrast between the robustness of the voice of the chaffinch and the slender notes of the redstart destroyed all resemblance. The redstart's is a thin song, but there is something brisk and wild in its tone that gives distinction. The first notes seem to be uttered with ease; the last notes sound as if they caused the bird a little effort and uncertainty. I have once heard the song as far north as Sutherland before the end of April.

There is one aspect of the redstart that differs from that of all these April-coming songbirds. None of these are brilliant in plumage; their beauty is quiet rather than gay: the plumage of the male, with the exception of the blackcap, is the same as that of the female, and does not alter much, if at all, after the breeding season is over. But the cock redstart has colours that arrest the eye: he is indeed one of the most beautiful of our birds; and it is a plumage of the breeding season; afterwards comes an eclipse that places him more nearly on a level with the female; but in all redstarts the patch of reddish colour on the tail coverts, from which they get their name, is constant.

Now we come to the nightingale – the most renowned of all songbirds; time-honoured and famous: poets ancient and modern have paid their tribute to it; its praise is in every mouth. Therefore no one can write of the nightingale with intimacy; to attempt to do so would seem an impertinence; as if one were to say that Homer was one's own favourite poet. On the other hand, to write of the nightingale without saying something special or individual would be banality: and yet it is impossible in a book about birds to omit an account of it. One way out of the difficulty of being banal when dealing with a popular hero is to decry him, to take him down a peg, so to say; but this may involve being original at the expense of truth. There is something to be said truly in criticism of the nightingale's song, and it shall be said presently; but to make it clear that I do not find fault for the sake of being original, the praise shall come first, and in unstinted measure.

'Marvellous' is an epithet to be used very sparingly either of mankind or of birds; but the epithet may be conceded to the song of the nightingale. Let us suppose a lover of bird song to be walking, slowly, with ears alert, about an oak wood in the latter part of May. The big trees stand sufficiently apart to encourage plenty of undergrowth – thickets of thorn and of bramble, hazel, and perhaps some bushes of whin. He hears, one after another, various songs familiar to him – thrush, blackbird, garden-warbler, blackcap, willow-warbler, whitethroat, and others; he selects the song of each with pleased attention: suddenly he is struck – it is almost a physical impact – by notes of an energy, force and dominance with

which none of the others can compare. The song is
not a linked phrase, like that of the blackbird: it is
repetition of one set of notes; then a pause, and then
a different set of notes: in this the plan of the song
resembles that of the thrush. We cannot tell which
notes will follow a pause. 'Jug-jug-jug' is an expression
used to describe the most usual and typical notes. But
the supreme achievement of the nightingale is a loud,
clear, sustained note that fills the air. The best notes
of other birds, blackbird or blackcap, for instance,
come distinctly from the point where the bird utters
them, and seem to reach and terminate at the listener's
ear; but the supreme notes of the nightingale envelop
and surround us: so that we lose perception of the
point whence they proceed: it is as if we were included
and embraced in pervading sound.

I recall nothing in bird song that has an effect like
this, except the sustained vibrating joy notes of the
curlew. Unfortunately one may listen to a nightingale
for a long time without hearing this perfection: it
seems to be almost beyond the compass of some
of the birds; but wherever a nightingale sings, it
is worthwhile to wait and listen for this wonderful
note.

The nightingale sings abundantly in the daytime,
but according to my own rather casual observations
it falls silent and takes no part in the sunset chorus.
It cannot be that it fears, but perhaps it disdains, the

competition with other birds. Then an hour or so after the last thrush has descended from its song perch and the last robin has ceased to sing, the nightingales will begin to fill the night with sound. Fully to appreciate the song, it is best to get close to one bird under the most favourable conditions of night and surroundings. One such instance will serve as an example.

Two friends, one English and one American, each with knowledge and love of birds, were to spend two days with me in Hampshire in the latter part of May. To hear birds in song was the object of the visit. In the previous weekend I stood near my cottage and listened for nightingales. Time had been when, for some years, a pair had bred in the old chalk-pit close to me; but that time was no more. One year the male had been in full song day after day and night after night; then one night in mid-May there was a silence that was never broken there by a nightingale again: a stealthy and deadly cat, at which I never could get a shot, frequented the thickets of the chalk-pit that year: the nightingale, and also a tame thrush that had trusted me for four years and come confidently into the rooms, both disappeared. No other thrush ever took its place, and no other nightingale came to the chalk-pit. So now I had to listen afield. I heard two nightingales at some distance, one close to the village about a quarter of a mile away; the other even more distant. A week later my friends arrived. Nothing was to be heard near the village, and about ten o'clock in the evening we went to the more distant place; but no nightingales were to be heard there either. A sedge-warbler offered himself as substitute, or, it may be, simply mocked us, and we retired unsatisfied to the village inn, where, in default of sufficient room in the cottage my friends were to spend the night. There I left them, and to prevent future disappointment went in search of another nightingale in some place more remote from village cats. One bird was heard, and the place carefully noted, in a large wild park with oaks and thorns and brambles. The next night we went to the place; the bird sang; we crept close to it; no burglars fearing detection could have approached more cautiously or whispered more low. The moon was rising as we crouched and listened: the bird's song was the only sign of life: for some time we remained; the bird sang, and paused and sang; finally our American friend said, 'Let us go away quietly and leave it singing.' We withdrew as cautiously as we had approached, and the bird sang on. It was no better than many another nightingale, but once again there had been a moment that lives in memory. The trouble taken to find the bird one night, the satisfaction of finding it the next night, the success in getting close to it without disturbing it, the rising moon, the stillness of the night, the apparent solitude of the bird, the whole circumstances and setting, all combined to make this one song memorable.

The conventional nightingale of literature is taken from ancient legend: it postulates a doleful bird, a female, perpetually lamenting, even leaning its breast against a thorn to make its mourning more poignant; this has no more resemblance to the real bird than heraldic emblems have to real creatures. Not so does Wordsworth write of the nightingale:

> O Nightingale! thou surely art
> A creature of a fiery heart:
> These notes of thine – they pierce and pierce;
> Tumultuous harmony and fierce!
> Thou sing'st as if the God of wine
> Had helped thee to a Valentine;
> A song in mockery and despite
> Of shades, and dews, and silent night;
> And steady bliss, and all the loves
> Now sleeping in these peaceful groves.

That is the authentic nightingale; it explains too why, if the nightingale's song is the most marvellous, it is not the most loved of English bird songs.

Fallodon is too far north for nightingales – they do not come to the garden at Wilsford, nor within hearing of it. We desire them and regret their absence; but if we were asked to give up blackbirds and were offered nightingales in exchange, the answer would be an unqualified and unhesitating 'No'.

The nightingale's song has compass, variety and astonishing power; it arrests attention and compels admiration; it has onset and impact; but it is fitful, broken and restless: it is a song to listen to, but not to live with. Wordsworth, in the poem already quoted, explains this feeling; he goes on to describe and to express his preference for the cooing of the wood-pigeon to the song of the nightingale. Here are some of the lines:

> He did not cease; but cooed – and cooed;
> And somewhat pensively he wooed:
> He sang of love, with quiet blending,
> Slow to begin, and never ending;
> Of serious faith, and inward glee;
> That was the song – the song for me!¹

If Keats had not written the 'Ode to Autumn,' I should have felt that his 'Ode to a Nightingale' had more magic quality than any other poem that I know. It touches heights of poetry that the lines of Wordsworth on the nightingale do not attempt; but the ode is less close to the bird. There are one or two things in it that, judged as a description of the bird and its movements, would need care and pains for

---

1 It must be noted that Wordsworth calls the bird a Stock-dove, but the description is clearly that of the cooing of the wood-pigeon.

their defence; but as a poem it is so exquisite that there is not a word I should like to be changed.[1]

The digression into literature has gone far enough; and so has criticism of the bird. As with Shakespeare so with the song of the nightingale – when all the faults have been found and admitted, the thing remains wonderful.

[1] I have been privileged to see the MS. of Keats' ode, which is in Lord Crewe's possession. Keats first wrote 'Magic casements opening on the foam of *keelless* seas in faery lands forlorn.' This is the epithet that agrees best with magic casements and faery lands, but it drags upon the ear. Keats scratched it out and wrote 'perilous' instead: but it must have cost him something to sacrifice the sense of keelless.

Chapter IV

The Month of Full Song

In May we pass definitely from the bareness of winter to the luxuriance of summer. Hitherto we have been able to appreciate fully the change of the seasons. April is warmer than March, but it is yet a cold month: there are days in April when a maximum temperature of 70 degrees in the shade may be hoped for; but these are few, and when they come, the warmth is no more wasted upon us than a well-cooked hot dish is wasted on a cold and hungry man. There is no risk of satiety in April; there is time to appreciate the first green leaves on larch, hawthorn or chestnut; to note separately the appearance of each kind of spring flower, to welcome one by one with eye and ear the arrival of each species of summer bird. We keep abreast of the beauty of the season and feel adequate to and worthy of it. But in May we are overwhelmed. New green is spreading everywhere; flowering shrubs and trees and flowers of garden and field are far too abundant for separate notice; all those birds yet named in this book, and more than these, are in full song. Neither eye nor ear, nor outward nor inward sense of man is equal to it. Each of us can select for especial and particular enjoyment a few things: the tender green of young beech leaves; the scent in mass of whin; a glade of bluebells; a wide field of buttercups under the sun: but when we have done our best, we are yet oppressed by a feeling that we can but take in a small portion of the abundant beauty. There comes upon us also, not only a sense of abundance, but of haste; it is all passing; the leaves darken from day to day; luxuriance remains, but tenderness and delicacy are fleeting. It is only for a short time that new beech leaves are so soft that the wind stirs them without sound. In early spring we long to hurry the season; in May we would say to it, 'Stay! thou art fair.' And it cannot be stayed: ' 'Twere all as well to bid a cloud to stand.'

At such times we are grateful to the reluctant ash, whose buds are black and open so late; and to the walnut; for these are still bare when other trees are first thick and green. The ash and walnut remind us, then, that all is not yet fulfilment; that there is still some promise and prospect to which to look forward. Just as there are one or two trees that come into leaf later than all the rest, so there are a few birds whose arrival with us is later than that of the others. There are four of these that are common: the swift, the red-backed shrike, the turtle-dove and the spotted fly-catcher. The main arrival of these is not in April, but in May. Books say that the red-backed shrike has a song, but I have never heard it. A pair nested for several years in the cottage chalk-pit; but I never observed anything that in sound or manner suggested a song. On the other hand, careful observation of the spotted fly-catcher discovered the bird to consider itself singing. A pair nested every year in the creepers on the sides of the one-storey cottage. Not till May did they appear, and every May they were expected and looked for. In the fortnight after its arrival one bird, presumably the male, would sit on some perch on or about the roof and make a small warbling: the sound was inward and so minute that one almost needed field glasses to hear it – clear vision of the attitude, motions and manners of the bird helps the ear to collect the sound. Having been once noted, this little performance was observed in more than one succeeding year, but always in the first fortnight only after the bird's arrival.

The spotted fly-catcher seems to live entirely on insects that it captures in the air; it chooses as a perch a dead branch or a bare rail from which it can have a clear view and an unimpeded flight. Swifts and the swallow tribe live on insects taken in the air; but each capture is only an incident in the bird's continuous flight. With the spotted fly-catcher each insect is the object of a separate flight and pursuit – a sporting and expert method of taking its food. Other birds, chaffinches for example, may be seen to do the same thing with some particularly attractive and succulent insect, such as a Mayfly; but they are not so expert, and with them the practice is an exception and not a habit.

The spotted fly-catcher's plumage is dull, and the male and female are alike: it does not mind the presence of mankind, and its constant little sallies after insects are a pleasant part of the bird life of many a garden. When the young are fledged they are much in evidence, perched on some convenient place, such as the garden fence, waiting to be fed by the old birds. The young of a pair that nested in creepers by the garden door at Fallodon appeared in a row on the lawn-tennis net in the morning when they left the nest.

Though without charm of voice or plumage, the spotted fly-catchers would be missed from any garden where their presence has been familiar. After the young are fledged the old birds utter what I suppose is a warning note; for it is repeated constantly when one approaches, and suggests, not so much that they are afraid, as that they think it tiresome of anyone to come near while they have a family to feed.

In May, when all the summer birds are with us, and established in nesting-places and territory, the great dawn chorus is at its fullest and best. Unfortunately this wonderful opening of the day occurs at an hour when civilised man is either in sleep or suffering from the want of it. In the first case he does not hear the singing; in the second he is in no mood to enjoy it; is, in fact, not worthy of it. Wordsworth knew this well when he wrote in his best-known sonnet to 'Sleep':

> And yet do lie
> Sleepless! and soon the small birds' melodies
> Must hear, first uttered from my orchard trees;
> And the first cuckoo's melancholy cry.

His other references to the cuckoo that I recall are happy: shouting 'faint tidings of some gladder place'; 'I hear thee and rejoice'; but to the sleepless man it is 'melancholy'. Without sleep 'what is all the morning's wealth?' We become used to external sounds at night. A slight disturbance inside the room, the minute restlessness of a mouse, for instance, will destroy sleep; yet in London people sleep on while the traffic in the street roars outside their windows. In like manner the countryman sleeps through the dawn chorus of birds: or if he does wake and try to listen, it is but a struggle between the desire to hear and the impulse to sleep again. The dawn chorus is at its best between three and four[1] o'clock in the morning, when man's vitality is at its lowest and his spirit most depressed. Winter and summer alike he needs about the same amount of sleep and keeps the same hours. With the birds it is not so: in midwinter the small birds sleep from dusk to dawn, about fifteen hours; in midsummer only for about six hours; it is difficult to be sure that the nightingale and sedge-warbler sleep at all. And when birds wake it is in the highest vitality and spirits, which are expressed in united song before ever a morsel of food is sought by them.

The following passage written by my wife is the best description of a dawn chorus that I know, and may be appropriately quoted here:

It is worthwhile to wake early during these days, because of the dawn chorus. It opens with a few muted notes of thrush song. This sets the tits waking; they have no half tones. There are the sawing notes, the bell notes, the teasing notes, and the festoon of small utterance that belongs especially to the Blue.

But you can hardly pick out the individual songs before

[1] True time, not artificial 'summer time.'

the whole garden is ringing. There is the loud beauty of the thrushes. Seemingly further away, and in remoter beauty, comes floating the blackbird's voice. The notes are warm, and light as amber, among the sharper flood of song.

The dawn chorus is like a tapestry translated into sound. The mistle-thrush, with merle and mavis, perhaps the rounded note of an owl, these stand out chief figures in the design. All the others make the dense background of massed stitches; except the wren; he, with resounding scatter of notes, dominates the throng.

Then as suddenly as it arose, 'this palace of sound that was reared,' begins to subside. One or two thrushes persist. The greenfinch goes on with his two modes of single utterance. Perhaps a linnet continues his husky song. He can be heard now. Then the sun rising flushes the water-meadows, and the snipe start drumming ... The grass is all bent and straggled with its weight of cold dew.

It seems to me that the summer birds do not make so much of the sunset as they do of the dawn, but the evening chorus is upheld by resident birds, especially blackbirds and thrushes, and it is well to listen to it and note the close: there comes a time when all have ceased except thrushes and robins; then the thrushes stop and robins are left singing alone to end the day.

In May there is a new interest in hearing the songs of birds about the garden and neighbourhood of a

country home: in early spring the songs of resident
birds mean the renewal of life in a new year: in
April we note the first songs of summer birds as
announcement of arrival, though the bird may be still
on its journey; but in May the continuance of the
song day after day in the same place is an assurance
that the bird has a territory, a mate and a nest. Year
after year we expect a pair of blackcaps or garden-
warblers or other species to occupy again the same
territory as in previous seasons, and to nest in it. At
Wilsford, for instance, there is one part of the garden
where a blackcap is expected to arrive in April and to
sing through every May and June: a pair of willow-
warblers occupy one small orchard every season: it is
not enough to hear blackcaps and willow-warblers as
we walk in the country: there is one blackcap and one
willow-warbler that are to be part of life at home for
each season. So it was at the Hampshire cottage: not
all the blackcaps in the neighbourhood would have
been full compensation for the absence of the one
pair that were due to the chalk-pit and that never
failed. Thus in May we are pleased, not merely with
the song of a particular species, but we listen to an
individual bird with peculiar satisfaction. There is in
such instances something of the satisfaction of personal possession, and yet the interest of observing a
wild thing, free from all restraint, is unimpaired. Those
only who have this feeling know how much the

enjoyment of a garden is enriched and enlivened by it; and to those who have it not, the pleasure of it cannot be conveyed. But as with all pleasures of the sort, those who encourage and cherish this one give hostages to fortune. Our own special birds may be faithful to the nesting territory while they live, but some mischance may befall them during their long journeys and absence, or some evil thing may destroy them while they are with us. In one little piece of rough ground near a small pond at Fallodon there were always a garden-warble, a whitethroat and a sedge-warbler to be heard: the last was the only bird of its kind that was ever to be heard in this garden. Three years ago the sedge-warbler was in full song and chatter in May; then came a day of ominous silence, and I have never heard the bird or one of its kind there since. A hawk was at the time taking brood after brood of young waterfowl, and probably it took the sedge-warbler. The garden-warbler and the whitethroat still come every year: I sit and listen to them with satisfaction, but I miss the sedge-warbler that was for so many years associated with them in that place.

In the two months from the end of the third week of March to the end of the third week of May, there is accomplished the most rapid contrast of the year: a few summer birds may have come to us before this period begins, but with these few exceptions it includes the arrival of all our summer birds; the transition from cold to warmth; from dark bare branches to thick green trees. It is well sometimes to heighten the enjoyment of the best days of May by recalling some typical day of the preceding March. An instance may be taken from salmon-fishing in spring. The angler had spent a week on the river Spey in March, and one day in particular dwelt in his mind. As far as sport was concerned, it had not been unsuccessful, and when that is so, no stress of weather can destroy his pleasure. About three o'clock in the afternoon, bent on turning a day of fair into one of really good sport, he was advancing into a broad strong stream to wade as far out as the current would allow and as deep as he dared to go: a blizzard met him full in the face, with buffeting wind and blinding multitudes of snowflakes: the deciduous trees were stark and bare: in that stern week there was little song in the woods even of thrush or wren: on the river, apart from dippers, the only lively and constant evidence of birds was the presence of black-headed gulls and oyster-catchers. The latter birds are very noisy at that time of year. They are often in parties of three, and the exceeding restlessness gives the impression that two birds are perpetually trying to escape from the presence of a third, whose company is tedious and unwelcome; but whether this is an intrusive male or a superfluous female, I cannot say, for the sexes are alike in plumage, and I have not observed the birds to fight, as rival males probably would do.

Such were the conditions and the aspect of the place in March. In the latter part of May the angler was there once more; he had chanced on a cold week of March; it was now one of the warm weeks of May. The river was still broad and in fair order, though not so full as in March: the fishing had declined from good to fair: but it was sufficient to keep him keen and at work. There came a moment when the contrast with March was thought of and enjoyed. Again he was wading deep in the stream; behind him were some acres covered with whin, broom, wild raspberry and other wilful growths: in these thickets were some sedge-warblers and whitethroats, and their songs came to him repeatedly; the sun shone warmly, the broom was coming out, but the whin was in full flower and fragrance; a light breeze brought the wonderful scent about him. Is the whole air ever so wonderfully and gratefully fragrant as when it is pervaded by the scent of whin? New-mown hay or a bean-field in flower are rare delights, but the flower of whin is best of all. The scent is fresh and invigorating, and yet so rich and luscious that it suggests apricots: it is as if the apricot had been designed in order to transmute part of the excellence of the scent of whin into something that could be perceived by another sense than that of smell. At any rate, both the scent and the fruit have this in common, that each is only to be known to perfection when warm in a hot sun. The whin is suited to the British climate; it needs no hot weather to enable it to flower and ripen its seeds. A cool summer does not discontent it; but it cannot endure extreme cold, and is grateful for our mild winters: it is essentially a plant for a Gulf Stream climate. A stray flower of whin may be picked, so far as anything so prickly can be picked at all,[1] on most bushes in every month of the year; but it is in May that every bush of whin is a glorious blaze of colour. Later in the summer, on a warm day there is a sporadic ticking noise amongst the whins: it is the opening of the dry seed-pods.

But I have now digressed enough. It is difficult when writing of outdoor things to keep to one subject, even that of birds – the world, as Robert Louis Stevenson says, 'is so full of a number of things' – and it is time to return to the proper subject of the book. The oyster-catchers are still about the river in May, but they are less noisy and restless than they were in March. They have eggs to attend to. These are laid on shingle, with no attempt by the bird to hide them; but their pattern is so cunningly devised that the whole bed of shingle is their concealment.

To the bird life on the river, May has now added

---

1 It was once said of one who loved the country, as a tribute to the strength and extent of her affection for outdoor things, that 'she not only could but habitually *did* pick gorse (whin).'

two common species of summer birds – terns and sandpipers. The flight of terns is graceful, light and airy, a delight to the eye; the voice is harsh. Sandpipers give an impression of happy affection, as a pair flit about together, piping pleasantly as if each enjoyed the other's company. My recollection is that both birds pipe; but there are details like this that one may for years take for granted, and then suddenly question with a desire for more particular observation.

To all this must be added the full song of woodland birds; the long vibrating notes of curlews, the first fresh green of deciduous trees and geans with their abundant delicate white flower. Year after year all this loveliness for eye and ear recurs: in early days, in youth, it was anticipated with confidence; in later years, as the season approaches, experience and age qualify the confidence with apprehension lest clouds of war or civil strife, or some emergency of work, or declining health, or some other form of human ill may destroy the pleasure or even the sight of it: and when once again it has been enjoyed we have a sense of gratitude greater than in the days of confident and thoughtless youth. Perhaps the memory of those days, having become part of our being, helps us in later life to enjoy each passing season. In every May, with the same beauty of sight and sound, 'we do beget that golden time again'.

Chapter V

JUNE AND JULY

From Full to Least Song

The account of May has been comparatively short, because the description of the many songs that are at their best in May has been given in previous chapters. We think of June as a summer month, but judged by average temperature there is much advance still to be made before we get full summer warmth.

The study of statistics always corrects current notions of weather, and it is interesting to note the progress made from cold to warmth: it is very uneven. By the first of January the northern hemisphere is turning to the sun, but till the middle of February there is practically no advance in warmth: by the end of February the gain from the coldest days in mid-January is only about 2 degrees. In March the further gain is about $4\frac{1}{2}$ degrees. April lags behind March with a gain of only $4\frac{1}{5}$ degrees. In May comes the greatest change in any one month, for the average temperature rises about 8 degrees; but in June there is a further gain of $4\frac{2}{5}$ degrees: thus June, if judged by quick rising temperature, is as much a spring month as March or April, and the singing in the first part of this month is as good as at any time of the spring. Yet early in June, before summer has fairly come, we note that song is beginning to fail. The nightingale, absorbed in the labour of feeding its young, ceases to sing. After the end of the first week in June the falling-off in nightingale song is very rapid. The blackbird leaves off singing before June is over. When I left Fallodon on the 11th June 1926, the blackbirds were in full song – so vigorous were they every evening that it was hard to believe that the end was so near. They were singing as if with assurance of weeks of song yet to come. On the 26th June I returned, and from then to the end of the month there was no blackbird singing in the gardens, though once or twice a feeble and declining note was to be heard in the neighbouring woods. This is quite according to rule, but no general statement about birds can be made to which there will not be exceptions. Anyone who cares to observe or listen to birds with the object of collecting instances to disprove general rules may have considerable success. One instance of blackbirds singing well on into July has already been given, but blackbirds in normal conditions go into the moult in July, and no one who has seen what a pitiful and deplorable object the smartest cock blackbird can become in the moult would expect a song from it.

On the other hand, I have noticed in certain birds a revival of song in the latter part of June, which is continued into July. In the Hampshire chalk-pit, where a pair of blackcaps nested every year, it was noticeable that the song would become very infrequent for some days in the latter part of May or early in June. The birds were then engaged in feeding the young: while this was so, whether before or after the young left the nest, there was little time or energy to be spent on song. Then would come a time in the latter part of June when the chalk-pit blackcap repeated his song from dawn to dusk. I have noticed in the same place a similar slackening and revival of song on the part of the wren and the chiff-chaff. Except in the case of the wren, the late June song was not quite so vigorous as it had been before the young were hatched; but it was the full spring song and not the fainter resumption of song that is heard late in summer before the birds leave us. If the number of times that each bird repeated its song in one day had been counted, the figure would, I am sure, have seemed incredible. I have made the same observation in the case of the garden-warbler, and no doubt close attention would extend it to other species.

The slackening of song while the birds are hard-worked in rearing the young does not need explanation: when the young require no more care the old birds are liberated; their energy and vitality are still great, and till these are repressed by the moult, the male has little else to do than to indulge the impulse to sing.

One observation on the chalk-pit blackcaps will illustrate the point. The nest was found when it was still only a beginning; the male helped in the building of it, and this work caused no great diminution of his song: the nest was in a small thicket of wild-rose, and the cock bird, after having made his little contribution to the nest, would sometimes sing in the rose bush before he left in search of more material. He took his share of sitting on the eggs: he was not observed to sing while actually himself sitting on the nest,[1] but his

1 An expert English ornithologist has told me that he heard and saw a garden-warbler sing while sitting on the eggs, and I have heard

song was pleasantly frequent till the young were hatched. Then he became almost silent. Early one morning from my bedroom – it must have been about a week after the young were hatched – I heard the blackcap singing repeatedly. I guessed with foreboding what had happened and went to the nest. It was empty: the young had been safe, but not ready to fledge, the day before; and now in the early morning something hostile, probably jackdaws, had taken them. How the female blackcap was affected there was no evidence to show, but the male gave the impression of joyous liberation and high spirits.

This incident belongs properly to the chapter on 'Nests', but it is inserted here as being the most apt example known to me of this revival of song after the young have ceased to be an occupation to the male parent. This spurt of song on the part of certain individual birds does not, however, compensate for the general decline of song, which is very marked in the latter part of June.

June is not so good a month as May for observing birds: in early May the leaves on many trees are still small, and some trees are bare, even when all the summer birds have arrived. It is the one period of the season when all our birds are present and most visible. Before this, though the trees are bare, the stock of

that the same thing has been observed of some other species of bird in North America.

birds is incomplete: later the thick summer growth of leaves and herbage hides them. Some ten yards in front of the Hampshire cottage was a row of poplars, not the so-called black Italian poplar that comes late into leaf, but an earlier-leafing sort: the row was broken in the middle by an old walnut and a lusty young ash: bird after bird, hidden among the leafy poplars, would expose itself on the bare branches of the walnut or the ash. Thus sitting in the garden doorway in the first half of May with a pair of field glasses, it was often possible to get an exceptionally good view of birds otherwise not easily seen. In the early days of May the utmost use should be made of field glasses. In June it is summer 'and the green is deep,' and birds, though audible, are less easily seen. There is also great confusion to the eye now, owing to the numbers of young birds that are fledged. This is especially so with the warblers, of which the difference of plumage is often sufficiently indistinct even in adult birds.

In July, when so many songs have ceased, it is worthwhile to note the birds that still continue in full song. Larks, wrens and yellow-hammers have been familiar to us in the earlier months, and we hear them still; but there are some minor songs to which, though they began weeks ago, we now have time to give special attention. Three of these are buntings, that come into song later than the yellow-hammer. The cirl-bunting is the best singer of the three; it is a bird that is common only in certain districts. The song resembles the first part of that of the yellow-hammer, but is fuller in tone; it has, however, not the variety of the yellow-hammer's song; it suggests to me the ringing of a small electric bell of pleasant tone and good quality of sound, but monotonous. My first hearing of it was an incident not to be forgotten. I was bicycling back from the Test to the Itchen Valley; I had taken field glasses, for the object of the ride was to look out for birds. I left the Test Valley at Stockbridge and had reached the turn beyond Lainston, where a side road makes a short-cut to the left to Harestock: at the turn I missed the field glasses and knew that I must have left them at the inn at Stockbridge, some miles distant: the road has many ups and downs, and it is no pleasant matter to retrace miles just travelled with the knowledge that after retracing them one must come back over them again. The consciousness that nothing but one's own carelessness is to blame makes the process exasperating. The impulse is to take it out of oneself by exercise, as if punishment of the body were some compensation for forgetfulness of the mind. One is eager to get back to the starting point as soon as possible, and thus obliterate the loss of time and temper caused by the affair. There was no dismount till Stockbridge was reached: there I laid hand on the glasses, remounted immediately, and took the hill on the Winchester road out of Stockbridge without getting off. No mean performance for a Member of Parliament in the middle of the sedentary session in days when there were no change-gear bicycles. At the very spot where I had missed the glasses and had resolved that I must go back for them, I heard a song new to me. In a moment there was a dismount, and the glasses were out of their case; the bird was sitting on the top of one of the bushy yew trees that are so common in hedges in chalk country, and I was looking at and hearing a cirl-bunting; pictures of the bird were well known to me, and the lemon yellow and chocolate colour about the head made it unmistakable. This was more than compensation for time lost: indeed, hearing the song of the bird at that very spot seemed like a reward for the resolution taken there, though the spirit of wrath in which I had ridden those extra miles to Stockbridge and back had merited no such gracious occurrence. Afterwards I came to know the bird as common in that district, and W. H. Hudson so describes it in *Hampshire Days*.

The cock reed-bunting is very handsome, and the birds are common on ground that suits them, such as chalk-strewn water-meadows and reed and sedge

growths. At Wilsford, where water-meadows adjoin
the garden with no fence to separate them, the
reed-bunting is a garden bird. In spite of his noble
appearance the reed-bunting has rather a paltry song:
it suggests to me the ascent of steps, the first two
or three being mounted sedately and the last taken
trippingly. In the plenitude of song in May and early
June the reed-bunting's contribution would not be
missed, if he happened to be absent or silent, but in
July by a chalk-stream I should miss him very much;
there he prolongs the season of song. The regard felt
for his song is an example of how valuable the
insignificant may become when our attention is given
to it, and it is a part of pleasant associations. The
reed-bunting is very conspicuous, and places himself
well for observation: when his song has given notice
of his presence, it is worthwhile to look at him through
field glasses.

It is not altogether kind to write much or tell the
whole truth about the corn-bunting – his person or
his song. The tendency of buntings is to be robust
rather than slender, but the corn-bunting is the cart-
horse among them all. He has the habit, too, of
sometimes taking a short flight with legs hanging
down, as if it were too much trouble to tuck them up
neatly in flight like other birds: this adds an impression
of slovenly disposition to clumsiness of body. Though
the largest of our four common buntings, this bird is

the least beautiful in plumage. The males of the other kinds all have some distinction or vividness of colour. The male corn-bunting is content to be as dull as his mate, who in turn is duller than other females of this tribe.[1] For a perch the bird prefers telegraph wires or a wire fence. Corn-buntings must have been pleased when the abomination of wire took the place of green hedges or honest posts and rails grown and made on the country estate. I can even imagine that corn-buntings *like* barbed wire. On wire then, by preference, the corn-bunting will perch and grind out the noise that is his song. This suggests to me the sound of two hard pebbles triturated one against the other. There is neither melody nor pleasant pattern in his song. On the Hampshire and Wiltshire downs, where there are plenty of telegraph wires and where wire fences are sadly on the increase, it is impossible in midsummer to miss the corn-bunting and his 'song'. He thrusts himself upon our notice. I cannot think of one point in which the corn-bunting is not inferior. Even the egg is less remarkable than are those of buntings generally. Yet at last, in spite of the inferiority of the corn-bunting, of which the bird itself is so completely unconscious – for its whole demeanour is that of self-satisfied content – one gets a sort of humorous affection for it.

1 'Dull' is used comparatively. The nature of feathers is such that if considered closely, even the bird of dullest plumage is beautiful.

Three common sounds of courtship there are that continue noticeably in July – those of the wood-pigeon or cushat, the stock-dove and the turtle-dove. It is hard to say positively when the wood-pigeon and stock-dove do not coo: they begin early in the year: in the mild winter of 1924–25 they were heard at Fallodon in December and January. The cooing of the wood-pigeon is exceedingly soothing; it does indeed speak 'comfortable words'. For a poetic description of it I would refer to the whole passage in Wordsworth's lines to a 'Nightingale', of which part has already been quoted. It is one of the redeeming features, indeed a real distinction for London, that the wood-pigeon can be observed there tame as well as free. It is the largest of our pigeons, and very beautiful; it walks busily and bulkily about the grass in the parks; there is an odd look in its eye that suggests perpetual astonishment. I have never seen one grow tame in the country in normal conditions; perhaps because it is a favourite object for everyone who shoots and because every farmer's hand is against it. Wood-pigeons are black-listed because of the damage done when they feed in large numbers on crops of tender green and of grain. It would be very sad if the race ever became extinct, and of this happily there seems to be no danger.

My wife once reared by hand a wood-pigeon that was hatched under a tame dove. It would feed readily and eagerly from the lips. For a time it remained tame and without fear, and it liked to be caressed; in August it was put into an aviary; there its native wildness began to assert itself – it would retreat to one end of the aviary and thence fly with force against the wire at the other end, as if it hoped by the impetus of a long flight to break through and get away. This was not from fear, for the bird did not flutter when we entered; it made these violent flights when no one was near; we could hear them from a distance: they were not caused by fear, but by sheer impulse to fly. Gradually the bird grew less tame and would not let itself be touched, nor would it feed from the hand. So it passed the winter; from having been the tamest it became the wildest bird in the aviary. Its head was sometimes scarred from the deliberate flights against the wire. It was let out, and for a time it came for food that was placed for it on the top of the aviary, and it frequently visited the garden; and though it flew away when approached, it was recognisably tamer than its kind, perching in a cherry tree close to the windows of the house. Eventually it was merged in the wild stock, and although in July a wood-pigeon would sometimes fly low over the garden, we ceased to be sure of its identity. Of many birds of other species thus reared by hand, I have never known one that showed such abhorrence of confinement even under the enlarged conditions of an aviary. This example confirmed the common saying that the wood-pigeon cannot be tamed. Other birds that are brought up to regard a human being as a foster parent remain contented and attached.

The stock-dove's coo is not so attractive: it is bumpy rather than smooth; the bird is smaller than the wood-pigeon, and has not got the white ring nor the white markings on the wings; but the iridescence of the feathers on the neck is very beautiful when there is an opportunity of seeing the bird close. It seems to me that the stock-dove has increased considerably at Fallodon within my memory, but it may be that I took little note of the birds when I was young; or perhaps I mistook them for farm pigeons, which I was early taught to distinguish on the wing from wood-pigeons, to avoid shooting the tame birds.

In 1924 two apparently wild stock-doves discovered the grain on which the waterfowl at Fallodon are fed. They appeared in late summer, and came regularly to the evening feed, and soon grew tame. It was interesting to note the difference between their manner of feeding and that of the waterfowl. The grain is scattered dry over a considerable area. The waterfowl move as they feed, eating a grain here and another there, and so forth; the stock-doves picked up every grain within reach before moving. A pair of Chiloe wigeon, which were quite peaceful with the other waterfowl and the moorhens, showed the most intolerant animosity to the unoffending stock-doves, chasing them so that they took refuge in the upper branches of an overhanging beech tree; thence they would fly lightly down on to another part of the grain area and feed, till the Chiloe wigeon again discovered their presence. After a few weeks the stock-doves came no more, but about the same time in 1925 and 1926 one bird has appeared occasionally, showing the same manners and degree of tameness, and its presence has immediately provoked the same pair of Chiloe wigeon.

The turtle-dove is not a resident bird, and its notes are therefore looked forward to as a sign of arrival. This bird, I think, it must have been that suggested to Tennyson 'the moan of doves in immemorial elms'. The sound is like a crooning, with something of tenderness and affection in it. It is associated most pleasantly with warm still summer days in the South of England; there it is, part of the summer, which would be very incomplete without it. The bird is quiet in its ways, but its plumage is rich in colour when it can be seen close at hand: and the row of white spots at the end are very conspicuous when the tail is spread in flight. Turtle-doves as I know them in Hampshire and Wiltshire are fond of sitting on fields that are fallow and where the earth is exposed: presumably they find there some kind of food specially suitable to themselves.

While there is a continuance of certain songs in July, the ceasing of song is very noticeable. From the middle of June to the middle of July is the period of greatest diminution of song. In July we hear the last of the spring song of thrush and robin. To listen to the last of either of these two birds is not, however, so melancholy a matter as to hear the last blackbird's song. The robin and the thrush will be heard again soon: the blackbird will not be heard till February: the leaves must change colour and fall, the days get dark and short and then lengthen again; the worst severity of winter must be endured before we hear those moving notes once more.

Besides the birds already named which continue in full song in July, there are three others whose notes abound in English gardens – linnet, greenfinch and goldfinch. There are neither linnets nor goldfinches about the garden at Fallodon, but at Wilsford all three are abundant, and so they were at the Hampshire cottage. The song of the linnet needs close attention in order to hear the quality of some of its notes, which otherwise might pass unappreciated: it is well also to look at the cock bird through field glasses. The linnet is thought of as a brown and not a brilliant bird; and so it seems as usually visible to the naked eye. A mature cock linnet, however, in his best plumage is very handsome, with glowing pink on breast and forehead.

So, too, the cock greenfinch is a fine bird – green as a parrot may be green, and with a touch of yellow. His song is made up of various chirpings, but it has one typical drawn-out note that is always to be recognised as unmistakably that of a greenfinch. This sounds like 'eeze' or 'breeze'; and I think of it as a welcome suggestion on sultry hot days. The greenfinch is a real grosbeak, with strong mandibles that make short work of the hips of sweetbriar and wild-rose in autumn.

Goldfinches are happily very common in all chalk-strewn valleys that I have known, and doubtless in many other places. There were twelve nests in one season lately in one Hampshire garden of no unusual size; they make liveliness in July, when so many other birds are becoming dull. They are restless, always flitting about, and the fine gold on the wings is conspicuous as they fly: they are thus lively to the eye both in colour and in movement: and the young birds have this conspicuous yellow on the wings, so that they contribute to the vividness of the charm from the moment they are fledged, though their heads are plain and without the rich crimson of mature goldfinches. The song is rather trivial, a tinkling sound, but happy; and as the birds are so constantly on the move, now in one place and now in another, the garden is always being enlivened by them. Indeed, goldfinches give a touch of lightsomeness to the heaviest day in July. They suggest to me what the ash does among trees. July is the month in which to appreciate the ash. When the leaves of oak and beech are dark, impenetrable to sunshine, and stiff, almost stubborn, to the breeze, then observe a fine ash. The leaves are graceful on long stems, and are stirred by a gentle air, and the foliage is so open that the light seems rather to permeate and be welcome than to be excluded. With the early spring green and bright autumn colours of other trees the ash does not compete; even in bareness its stout branches tipped with black buds are without the grace of other trees in winter; but in midsummer it has a gracious presence. No day in midsummer can be unrelievedly heavy if there are goldfinches in the garden and ash trees in the field beyond.

Chapter VI

AUGUST AND SEPTEMBER

The Decline of Summer

The shooting and the stalking seasons begin in August, but, except for this, these two months are to me the least interesting of the year. It is still summer, but the days are getting perceptibly shorter and the weather a little cooler. Before August is over there will be a suggestion that a fire would be comfortable after dinner. Gardens are very gay, but the excitement and freshness of early summer flowers are gone. The best roses now are inferior in size and abundance to those of June or early July. The first great blow of roses and the lime-flower mark the climax of the year, and both are over. There is still abundance of colour to come, but there is less spirit in it all. Phloxes are beautiful, but there is something tired in the scent of them. I like it because it reminds me somehow of old books, and some phloxes look well in a library against a background of leather bindings; but I do not look forward to all the luxuriance of August as I do to the flowers of the earlier season. What place has *Hyacinthus candicans* in our affection compared with lilies of the valley? Trees are now sombre, and the colours of autumn are not yet upon them.

These are very silent months for birds; even those that sing through July do not continue through August; though several are to be heard early in the month. There is nevertheless some interest even now, for the last of the spring songs can be heard to overlap the first of the autumn. The robin has been silent since early in July, and he begins again early in August. His first autumn song should be noticed before the last indefatigable wren has decided to rest its voice and before the yellow-hammer's song has ceased. Willow-warblers will utter a subdued and infrequent song – its 'shadow' song, as a friend aptly calls it – but unmistakably authentic. A casual starling will give entertainment by some pleasant, if fragmentary, whistling. Thus even in the first weeks of August birds that have by silence given notice that the season of courtship and nesting is over, are now announcing that a new season has begun.

The terms 'spring' and 'autumn' song have been used without close definition, and it is not easy to define them. By 'spring' song is meant the song which accompanies the breeding season, and which may be continued without any marked break of silence well into summer. By 'autumn' song is meant the song which begins again in late summer or early autumn, after some weeks of silence. Thus the robin begins his autumn song in August after a very marked period of mid-summer silence: there is a distinct break between the 'spring' and 'autumn' songs. But having recovered his voice in August, he will, in a mild winter, continue without interruption till the end of next June. In this case, how can we tell when the 'autumn' song ceases and when the 'spring' song begins? Is there any real distinction between the two, except one of degree? For as the pairing time approaches the voice becomes more vigorous.

Again, the willow-warbler, wistfully, and the chiff-chaff more confidently, have begun to sing before they leave us in September. Do they continue their song in their warm winter quarters? If they do, the same question posed for the robin is applicable to them. All I have been able to observe is that some willow-warblers and chiff-chaffs are singing when they leave us and also when they arrive. Do they have one song in the year, or two? We know that they have a period of silence in midsummer; have they another in winter?[1] This leads to the larger question: What is the reason, cause or origin of song? The answer is difficult and complicated.

A philosopher of great repute in his lifetime is reported (whether truly or not, I do not know) to have said that the explanation was very easy: birds sang when food was abundant and their vitality high; when weather was cold and vitality low, they did not sing. An imaginary dialogue will test this sweeping and facile statement.

Let us suppose one speaker, *A*, to have stated this theory in conversation with another, *B*.

B – 'But August and September are the two months of all the year when insect food, fruit and seeds and grain are particularly abundant and available to birds; yet these are the months of least song.'

A – 'All living creatures that, like birds, have a special period of the year devoted to reproduction of their species, are exhausted and depressed after this period is over: it is, for instance, so with red deer amongst mammals, and with salmon amongst fish; and in these cases it is the males that suffer most. I understand also that birds moult and change their

---

1 This question recurs in the next chapter as relevant to another point than the one considered here.

feathers in midsummer, and that this is an exhausting process: the male birds suffering particularly from these causes have not recovered sufficiently in the months that you mention.'

B – 'But why should the thrush begin to sing again in October with some frequency, while the blackbird does not? The blackbird is apparently as naturally vigorous a singer as the thrush, and when food is abundant for one, it is equally so for the other?'

A – 'I cannot answer that question with certainty. It may be that the moult of the blackbird is more severe than that of the thrush: the blackbird, therefore, does not recover sufficiently to resume his song before winter is upon him, with cold and scarcity of food.'

B – 'Your answer is plausible, but nevertheless it seems to me strange that the robin, who is a most wretched object in his midsummer moult, should recover sufficiently to sing early in August, and the blackbird should not have recovered even in October. If food and warmth were really the cause of song, surely the resumption of bird song in late summer and autumn would be more general than it is, for in fact it is more exceptional than general. How is it, further, if food and warmth are the decisive factors in song, that the mistle-thrush begins to sing in midwinter?'

I cannot on his own theory invent a plausible answer for *A* to this last question, and the conversation shall cease. It must be conceded that scarcity of food in very hard winters stops birds from singing: a fair supply of food is essential to song, but it is not the cause of it. The Israelites could not make bricks without straw, but the presence of straw was not the reason why they made bricks.

Now let us test the theory that song is part of courtship and pairing, and is the expression of the excitement that belongs to this season. This theory fits the blackbird perfectly: to hear a blackbird sing before February is so exceptional that the bird cannot be said to have an autumn song. The song therefore begins when the instinct to pair is felt: it ceases as soon as the breeding season ends: it is in fact limited to that period alone. Of such birds as the blackbird it may therefore be said, with some hope of being accurate, that the desire to impress the female, the rivalry, the combativeness and the excitement that belong to this season, are the cause of song; but if we proceed to make this statement universal, or even general, we get into difficulties. The robin will then become particularly inconvenient. Not only has he no thought of pairing in the autumn, but he will not tolerate a female near him. Each robin is then alone in its territory, and if another robin enters it, there is not love but combat, whatever the sex of the intruder may be. The result of some special observation of the habits of robins will be given in a later chapter; it will suffice here to say that the arrangement of territories and the frontiers of each is not finally settled without disputes. The autumn and winter song of the robin may therefore be considered due to proclamation of its territory, assertion of its right to it, and determination to defend it. This alone is enough to cause song, which is naturally intensified when the impulse of the breeding season is added. The robin is passionately territorial, and therefore our most persistent songbird in autumn and winter.

I suspect, though I have not confirmed this by observation, that the wren is also very territorial, and this would account for its autumn song.

On the other hand, birds which flock or leave their breeding territories in pursuit of food – chaffinches, for example, and the flocks of the finch tribe that gather in cornfields and about stack-yards – have no territorial impulse at this season, and therefore no song. The observation already made upon the different habits of thrushes at Wilsford and at Fallodon respectively tends to support this theory. In the south they, or some of them, seem to remain in the same places as in the breeding season, and there they sing in autumn: at Fallodon, where they all shift, though it may be only two or three miles to the coast, they are claiming no territory, and even where they are seen to be present they are not in regular song as they are in the south.

We have now fairly reached three conclusions:

1. Adequate food is essential to song, but does not by itself cause it.

2. The impulse of courtship is an invariable cause of song in all songbirds. They sing at this season, if they sing at all, and do it to the utmost of their power.

3. The territorial sense without any other motive can cause song.

Yet even now we are not comfortable with the conclusions. What is to be said about the autumn song of the starling? These birds sing a great deal. Several will sit together on the same branch; and in autumn and winter they are gregarious. There is no question of territory here; nor of pairing at this season. The only explanation I can offer is that starlings sing at this season because there is no reason why they should not. A further conclusion must therefore be added to include such birds as the starling, and it may be stated thus:

4. Some birds may sing from nothing but a sense of well-being when they are in good health, and not depressed by moulting or adverse weather.

In the period of courtship any form of excitement may produce an outburst of song. Thus, as has already been noted, a stone thrown into a reed-bed will start reed or sedge-warblers singing: perhaps the pheasant's habit of crowing at the sound of thunder or big guns may be considered relevant, though this habit is not confined to the breeding season.

The song in the season of courtship is, I think, more a song of challenge or triumph than of love. It may indeed be a veritable war-song. I once saw two wrens locked together in combat on the lawn; they were so fiercely engaged as to be indifferent to my presence. One was at last victorious: the defeated bird fled; the victor flew into the nearest bush and shook the air with song.

Perhaps the conclusion of the whole matter is that we should enjoy the song of birds without questioning too closely why they sing. Enjoyment may be impaired by teasing oneself with trying to understand.

Chapter *VII*

OCTOBER, NOVEMBER, DECEMBER

The Winter Birds

September all glorious with gold, like a king
In the radiance of triumph attired.

So wrote Swinburne; and in the North of England such fields as have not been laid away to grass and still have a harvest are bright with corn. In the highlands of Scotland in late September the mountain-ash leaves have turned. Where a burn flows hidden in a rocky channel, its course can be traced from a distance by the bright deep red here and there of single chance-sown mountain-ashes that grow upon the banks. In England, however, as far as the woods are concerned, September is a dull month, and the lines of Swinburne are descriptive, not of September, but of October. September, in spite of possible equinoctial winds, is generally a quiet and pensive month. Gardens are very bright with Michaelmas daisies, montbretia and gay flowers of many colours, and red admiral butterflies sit upon dahlia flowers; but growth is ceasing. Plant life seems to be lingering rather than growing: summer has ceased its effort and is contemplating the result; waiting, but ready to withdraw at the first intimation that winter is on its way from the north. Some time in October – it may be early or late in the month – imperative frost will come, and in one night the heliotrope will turn black and the dahlias will be wilted. They are carried away, and only bare earth remains where all was so luxuriant. In September it was still difficult to find the gardener when you sought him in the kitchen garden, so hidden was he by tall green growth of peas and other crops and by leafy fruit trees and bushes. Now, when digging the bare earth, he is as conspicuous as any tall object in an open level field. Of green crops there is little to be seen, except late cabbage and the hardy, tight-curled, frost-defying brussels sprouts. I imagine a touch of obstinacy in their flavour; and how immensely long is their season!

This year (1926) at Fallodon there were three days in October -the 2nd, 3rd and 4th – that were as hot by day and as warm at night as if it were midsummer. There are generally a few days in October that are very warm, but by the middle of the month we are left in no doubt that summer is over and that we are in another season. The woods, that for so many weeks have kept a steady sombre green, now revel in a riot of colour. Most beautiful of all are the common wild-cherry trees, the geans, so wonderful and so tender in colour that it would be almost indelicate to attempt to describe them. A few of our forest trees shed their leaves without any bright display; the ash and the sycamore do so; but most trees have an individual and distinct beauty of their own. Horse-chestnuts turn early to pale gold; the 'English' elms do this also, but much later. No tree in autumn is more noble and honourable than the beech. Its dark leaves at first turn yellow; but the last stage before they fall is rich dark brown. As in spring there should be a Sunday set apart for seeing the young green beech leaves in their first beauty, so there should be a 'beech Sunday' for the colours in autumn. At Fallodon in an average year this is the last Sunday but one in October; in the South of England it is the first Sunday in November. But the autumn dates seem to be more variable than those of the spring. In this year (1926) the leaves were very late in turning.

The most perfect October days are those after night frost, with clear blue sky and calm. On such days bright leaves drop singly; each falling peacefully in due course of nature to rest on the ground, below the very twig on which it budded and grew.

There are other days in October of merciless ravage, with gales and rain. It is, on the average, the wettest month of the year; and yet it has very many fine days. Probably the rainfall is due to heavy rain on a few days, and not to small falls on many days. On the north-east coast in October I have known three successive days of persistent rain from the north-east. Measured by rain-gauge, those three days would have kept up October's record as a wet month, though all the other days had been fine. The colour on the ground in autumn woods must be noticed, as well as the colour on the trees, especially the cream-coloured carpet of the fallen lime leaves.

If it be asked what all this has to do with birds, the answer is that the coming of autumn is an event too important and splendid to be noted only by movements of birds. October, however, is the month when birds give us most conspicuous notice of the change of season. Birds that do not breed in this country at all come here and show themselves:

> Sent in on winter's service to announce
>
>   .   .   .   .   .
>
> That the rough lord had left the surly North
> On his accustomed journey.[1]

---

[1] Wordsworth applies these lines to robins coming in from the woods to sing near his cottage, but they are particularly applicable to migratory birds that come to us from the north.

Birds such as woodcocks, wood-pigeons and gold-crests do not come into this category. Great numbers of them come from abroad to spend the winter with us, but some also breed here. We can see them at all seasons, and their presence is therefore not exclusively associated with winter.

On the coast there are in autumn and winter quantities of birds that have never been known to breed in Britain. The grey lag goose is the only one of the wild geese that breeds in the British Isles; but now there come to us Pink-footed, Bean and White-fronted – all of them being grey geese; to these are added brent and bernicle geese, golden-eye and long-tailed ducks; and a host of small shore-birds such as knots, turnstones, purple sandpipers, sanderlings and many others. Some of these breed in places not easily reached: the curlew sandpiper, for example. This little bird was long ago observed and identified as a visitor to our shores on its journey south; but it is only within living memory that its breeding-place in Siberia has been found and its egg has been seen by any British ornithologist. All these birds, however, and even some birds such as the bluethroat, which are not shore-birds, are commonly seen on or near the coast and tidal mud-flats. They form no part of our inland home life.

There are four winter birds familiar to us that are distributed all over the country, and of which not one pair remains to breed. These are fieldfares, red-wings, bramble-finches, and jack-snipe.

Fieldfares and red-wings are thrushes, and seem to be gregarious during their stay here. The 'chacking' note of the fieldfare announces its presence, and both it and the red-wing frequent hedges and presumably feed on the berries. I have seen fieldfares in enormous numbers in a large wood, where the big trees were far apart and the space was filled with wild hawthorn. On one day of cover-shooting the fieldfares would not leave the wood, and were flying hither and thither in the air in such numbers as to be confusing to eyes that were on the watch for pheasants and other objects of a cover-shoot.

The red-wing is a tender bird; it is one of the very first to suffer in hard weather; before any blackbird or song-thrush shows signs of distress, a red-wing may be found hopping feebly at the foot of a house wall, pining and disconsolate. This little bird – it is the smallest of our thrushes – is less capable than our own resident birds of feeding itself in snow and frost, yet, though it is almost too tender for our winter, it will not stay with us to nest, and disdains the softness of our summer. The red-wing has bright red colour on its sides, and this strikes us as being unusual in a thrush; for the others that are common here have no bright colours. One of the North American thrushes has red colour on the breast. The early settlers naturally called it 'Robin,' after our own robin redbreast that they knew so well. The name has taken root there. The population of North America greatly outnumbers that of the British Isles: I suppose, therefore, that to the majority of English-speaking people the name 'Robin' now suggests this thrush, which is a larger bird and no relation to the robin of Christmas cards, and of our folklore and legend.

The fieldfare has no bright colour like the red-wing: it is not quite so large and fine a bird as the mistle-thrush; but in variety of shades of colours it is the most beautiful of all our thrushes.

Bramble-finches are due to arrive in October: they appear in small parties or flocks. If it is a good beech-mast year, they may be seen in great numbers under beech trees. At Fallodon the beech-mast is a very uncertain crop. In some years the sharp three-cornered husks are nearly all empty: in other years they are plump with kernel. In a good year I have seen the road under overhanging beech trees whitened by kernels that the traffic had crushed. In one such year, when a hard winter came, there were immense flocks of bramble-finches busily feeding under the beech trees. In mid-winter I calculated that there were far more bramble-finches than there were birds of any other single species on the place. They were very conspicuous on the thin covering of snow under the trees.

We understand from coloured plates in bird books that the bramble-finch in the nesting season has a black head and neck. I have only seen it in winter plumage, when a careless glance might not distinguish a party of bramble-finches from chaffinches: a field glass would show the difference. There is, however, no difficulty in identifying bramble-finches as they rise in flight. When the wings open there is the appearance of a white stripe between them, which is very evident and destroys at once, even to the naked eye and at some distance, the resemblance to a chaffinch. The chirp, too, is distinct. Someone who was asked to describe a certain sound gave the bewildering answer that it was 'a noise like a nut'. To me the note of the bramble-finch has always been a 'nutty' chirp.

In the winter referred to above, the bramble-finches came into a wire enclosure where the waterfowl were fed with wheat. I caught a cock bird, and it seemed to me that with a pair of scissors, by carefully cutting off the fringe of each feather on the head and neck, the bird could be turned into breeding plumage. It may be that this change is brought about merely by natural fraying of the edges of the feathers; but this must be referred to those who have more scientific knowledge of changes of plumage.

Fieldfares, red-wings and bramble-finches, after finding refuge here from the severity of Scandinavian winters and enjoying the hospitality of our fields, hedges and woods, sometimes even of our gardens, never let us see an egg or give us a song. Why do they not stay to nest here? It may be that there is some food farther north that is specially needed for their young, and which is not so plentiful here: or it may be only that it is their established custom to go north to breed. But why do they not sing before they leave? I have seen fieldfares at Fallodon at the end of the first week of May: by that time all our resident birds are in song; many of these have been singing for weeks, or even months. But if the song of any of these winter birds is heard in Britain, it is but a fragment. Every year we are familiar with these three species; but unless we go abroad we live out our lives in England and never hear their song. Is this because they cannot sing the home song in any but their homeland? Our resident birds, when they begin their song, are in the country, perhaps even in the very territory where they intend to nest. Is the rule that the home song shall only be sung in the homeland[1] observed by the warblers that come to us from the south in April? It is not a sufficient answer to say that willow-warblers or chiff-chaffs sing in the South of France before they reach us. The individuals heard in France may be birds that expect to nest there. What

1 'Homeland' is here applied not to the country in which the warblers spend the greater part of the year, but to the country in which they were born and in which they mate and nest.

is needed as an answer is to be told whether individual willow-warblers or chiff-chaffs that nest in Britain sing in their winter quarters or on their journey to us. Many chiff-chaffs resume their song before they leave us in September: do these same individuals take their song with them on their journey south and continue it through the autumn and winter, while they are away from us? Or do they cease singing when they leave England and not begin again till they return in March or April to the nesting country?

I pass now to a fourth common winter bird – the jack-snipe. We are sometimes tantalised with reports that the jack-snipe has been seen in Britain at a time and under conditions that suggest breeding; but so far as I am aware the experts have never been satisfied that any jack-snipe has yet laid eggs in Britain. It is a very quiet little bird; I have never heard it utter; when disturbed it rises quietly without sound or fuss; there is something meek about its flight; even when shot at and missed it will settle again at no great distance, as if it could not believe that the shot was intended for anything so small as itself. It relies rather on concealment than on flight. I once found one crouching in the angle formed by the garden path and the edge of the turf. It sat still at my feet, and for a while I admired the purple feathers, not disarranged by shot or violent capture, on the back of a living and uninjured jack-snipe. When a hand was put down it flitted easily and lightly away, with an appearance of airy unconcern, over a tall privet bush and the garden fence, to settle, no doubt, a few yards off up a little watercourse running into the pond, near which it had been sitting. It is a pity ever to shoot it, for its body is too small to give satisfaction when cooked, and all its ways and manners seem to deprecate violence or injury.

October is the month when the coming of these common winter birds is most noticeable about our homes; but the movement of birds to us from the north begins long before our summer is over. In most years, on some day early in August, a bird flies up from the edge of one of my ponds: it is larger than the common sandpiper, and it utters a cry that is more sharp and piercing than that of the redshank; sometimes there are two or even three birds, and they may settle again, but generally there is only a single bird, and it flies away with its sharp and repeated cry and is heard and seen no more. It is a green sandpiper. This bird has not been proved to breed in Britain; the bird seen at my pond has not spent the summer here; August is too late for it to be going north; the bird is therefore on its way south. It is said that the first birds to come South from Northern breeding places are old males. Presumably they are birds that have not paired or have taken no part in rearing young: their strength has not been impaired by domestic cares;

they are free from home duties, and they come south before the young birds are ready for the journey or the breeding birds have recovered and are free. Probably this green sandpiper is an old male: I have come to look for the appearance of one early in August as the first notice at Fallodon of autumn migration and winter birds.

There are other winter birds, more rare, but which with luck one may see once or twice in a lifetime about a country home.

In some winters there is a rush of waxwings to Britain; their presence in numbers is then reported from many parts of the country. A few years ago a flock of about thirty spent two or three days round the ponds at Fallodon. I was unfortunately away from home, but a friend saw and watched them. They were feeding apparently on the red berries of Viburnum (water elder), which seem not to be a favourite food of our resident birds, for they are left on the bushes till quite late in the year. Mountain-ash berries, on the other hand, are taken as soon as they are ripe; especially by mistle-thrushes, whose harsh chuckle about a mountain-ash tree is one of the common sounds of early autumn. The waxwing, I suppose, gets its name from some peculiar bright red feathers that look like drops of sealing-wax on the wing. Waxwing is at any rate a shorter and more pleasing name than 'Bohemian chatterer,' which is the alternative.

Another winter bird, still more rare, I have seen only once. It was on a January afternoon, a Sunday; I was walking along a plain public road on my way to post letters: there being no postman on Sunday, we often had to do this, and it was looked upon as a somewhat humdrum business, for the post office was three miles away and the road commonplace. Suddenly my attention was aroused by the note of a blackbird; it was more than the ordinary alarm note which blackbirds give when disturbed: it was a note that suggested terror. The blackbird flew along the hedge and sought cover therein; after it came a bird of about the same size, with smooth flight and rather a long tail: this second bird lit in a small bare hedgerow tree in front of me, and gave me a clear and satisfactory view of a great grey shrike. It did not appear to me that the shrike was actually in pursuit of or seriously threatening the blackbird, and the terror of the latter at the mere appearance of the shrike was remarkable. A year or two later, when I was in London and could not get home, it was reported to me early in March that a great grey shrike was seen for some days in a plantation near the house. It frequented a spot where long-tailed tits were used to build every spring. One of these tits was found slaughtered while the shrike was about the place, and there was no long-tailed tit's nest in this plantation that year.

In *Fallodon Papers* an account is given of seeing a

woodcock arrive from over the sea on the coast of Northumberland, fresh and strong, on a still autumn day; but the fact that gold-crests cross the North Sea is one of the marvels of migration. An account of their doing this in vast numbers is given or quoted in Kirkman's book on British birds; their numbers are compared to snowflakes. We are told that in times recent, if measured by geological periods, there was no North Sea. The space now covered by its water was land, through which a great river flowed north to the Arctic Ocean. The Rhine was the head water of this river; the Thames was one of its tributaries. In that age the western migration of birds to Britain would be an easy and regular movement; presumably the change from land to sea was slow, and even the smallest birds developed, century by century, power of flight sufficient to carry them across the gradually widened stretch of water. In favourable weather they can do it with ease; in unfavourable weather they arrive greatly exhausted or perish in the attempt. Woodcocks pass on in numbers to Ireland, and there the instinct of their kind stops them. If any woodcocks have attempted to emulate Columbus and to cross the Atlantic, they have not returned, and have had no successors to whom they could transmit a disposition to deviate from the settled habit of the race.

Ocean currents and prevailing winds affect climate, so that where no mountain barrier stops them, birds can get as good a change of climate by going from east to west as from north to south. The plan of currents in the North Atlantic and the North Pacific seems to affect the respective coasts of the Old World and the New World in the same way. The warm Gulf Stream washes the north-western shores of the Old World; a cold current comes down the North-east coast of the New World. The result is that New York, comparable in latitude to Lisbon, has a winter more severe, beyond comparison, than that of Shetland. In the same way a cold current comes down the north-east coast of Asia, and the sea freezes in winter at Vladivostock; but if we trace the line of latitude west from Vladivostock to Europe, we find our pointer on the map passes a little, and only a very little, to the north of Rome. The Japan current in the North Pacific corresponds, I suppose, to the Gulf Stream in the North Atlantic, and has a similar effect on climate, of which the north-west coast of America gets the benefit. Thus, except where mountain ranges interfere, birds that breed in the east of a continent can get a mild winter by moving west, and in the winter the British Isles receive a westward as well as a southward movement of birds.

As May is the month of greatest rise, so is October the month of greatest fall in temperature: the drop in average mean daily temperature is 7 degrees. In November the fall is about 6 degrees. November is the month when trees get bare; winter birds continue to arrive; but in a normal year there is no great snow or frost in November, and the birds have an easy time, without severe cold or lack of food. We may even see swallows still lingering and not in distress early in November;[1] but they are in peril, for they have a long way to go, and a sudden change of weather may cut off their food supply on their long line of communications across the Continent.

Of bird sounds still to be mentioned is the noble hoot of the brown owl. It is not peculiar to autumn, but it is very noticeable in autumn and in winter, as Shakespeare knew very well:

> When icicles hang by the wall
>
> .   .   .   .   .
>
> Then nightly sings the staring owl,
>
> > Tu-whit;
>
> Tu-who, a merry note.

Poets invest the hoot of the owl with whatever feeling suits their mood or the context of the poem. Gray, thinking of it in the melancholy mood of evening by a churchyard, says:

[1] Five swallows were seen at Fallodon on the 3rd November and two on the 7th November this year (1926).

The moping owl doth to the moon complain.

And the hooting has often been regarded as bodeful. The normal hoot consists of one fine, smooth long note; then a pause of about four seconds; then a long note, quavering at first and ending smooth and full. Sometimes the bird will give the first long note without following it up by the quavering note, but this is a broken and imperfect performance. I have occasionally, when standing unperceived near an owl, heard it go on for some time uttering one plain but fine-toned hoot with very little pause. The hoot of the brown owl enriches our woodlands, and without it they would be seriously impoverished. If the owls have a period of silence when they may be expected to hoot, I become restless and anxious lest they should have left the place. The hoot is, I suppose, the note peculiar to the male bird when he is in vigour; it is often answered by another bird at some distance, and appears to be, like some bird songs, a proclamation of territory. A note which seems to be simply a call note sounds like 'ke-wick'; in the time when young owls are about it is sometimes repeated in a single tree, with such frequency as to be tiresome, if near the house.

So far as I know, the brown owl is the only one of our owls that hoots; and if this be so, it is a great boon to us that it is our commonest owl, and indeed that we have it at all. The mobbing of an owl by small birds raises one question that has always puzzled me. The animosity of little birds against the brown owl is intelligible enough: it is well for them to be in safe roosting places before the owl comes abroad; and whatever the hoot may convey to human ears, there is reason enough for it to suggest beak and talons and to be full of foreboding to small birds. But why, if they mob the owl at all, do they do it so seldom? The occurrence is well known. We are in the woods and are arrested by an excited chatter of small birds of different species, drawn by common interest towards one thick fir tree. If we approach the tree, or if we watch till the annoyance becomes intolerable to the owl, we see it fly from the tree: the small birds then pursue it with cries that express hatred and disgust. The brown owl and the small birds are in these woods every day, but we only see this mobbing very occasionally – a few times in a whole year: it is not reasonable to suppose that it is only on these few occasions that the other birds become aware of the presence of the owl. Why is it so seldom that they take any notice of it? Possibly the fuss begins by some small bird coming upon the owl unaware, and finding itself so close to it as to get a fright. The scared note of the small bird would draw the attention of other birds, who would assume that the owl had done something menacing, contrary to its habit in daylight.

This would be a breach of the custom of the woods, which enables small birds and brown owls to exist together in the same wood in peace during daylight. The birds would resent it and combine to shift the owl, knowing that it is not formidable to them by day.

The appearance of a hawk in the daytime causes abject terror as a rule: each bird cowers for safety; but now and then birds combine to mob a hawk, and of the circumstances that embolden them to do this I can suggest no explanation. Birds seem never to be indifferent to the presence of a hawk: they either cower from or mob it: but to the owl their attitude in the daytime is, as a rule, that of indifference, and why they should so very occasionally depart with such energy from this attitude it is not easy to divine.

In December the season passes from autumn into winter, and we may have a really good fall of snow. Snow is a wonderful event; the enjoyment of it is on no account to be missed. There is something exciting about new-fallen snow of any depth: everyone knows the exhilaration with which a dog races about and plays in new snow. I have seen a tame covey of partridges show the same emotion at the first fall of snow, and play in it with every sign of excitement and enjoyment.

To get up on a winter morning and find the landscape made white by a heavy, quiet fall of snow in the night is like the discovery of a new land. That same morning we must walk in the woods, especially in a young fir wood laden with snow. It is all so soft, so white and so silent. There is a sense of mystery in a snowy wood on a still day that can be felt but not described. This aspect will last only for a day or two, or it may be only for a few hours; the first wind will dispel that impression of mystery; the snow will be blown off the branches and the trees will cease to be great white forms of unusual shape, and will become trees again. It is to be hoped that when the wind comes it will be strong; then the snow in the open country will be blown into drifts and ridges and waves, with outlines and shapes of great beauty. It may even be that roads and railway will be blocked by drifts, and those who do not wish to go away may have a valid excuse for staying at home. Such is snow, if we are fortunate enough to be in the country when there is a big fall of it.

There are other interests in snow besides the mysterious beauty of it. In the garden you may see something at which you stop and gaze, as Robinson Crusoe did at the footprint on the sand. It is the track of a rabbit, baleful and unmistakable. A large garden, especially if shrubbery and rough ground be enclosed therewith, can seldom be kept quite free from rabbits: there is generally one rabbit left, believed to be the very last; but when this has been exterminated one more very last rabbit appears – *uno avulso, non deficit alter.* The first fall of snow often gives this information, and however confidently the gardener may believe the garden to be safe from rabbits, he will peruse the snow with care and anxiety.

In the woods outside there is much to interest and instruct us. We know better in snow than at any other time what has passed in the woods when we were not there to see it. Large, rather irregular marks show where a dog has been: The footmarks of a fox are regular, but give an impression that the motion was free and easy: a very tidy track shows where a stealthy cat has prowled. Rabbit tracks are so numerous as to make one fear for young trees, if the hard weather be prolonged; but a few rabbits will make tracks enough to suggest a multitude. The pattern of a hare's track is on the same plan as that of a rabbit, but is larger and more open; a squirrel's track is neater, for it is two pairs of footprints, the hinder ones close together side by side, the foremost also parallel to each other, but wide apart. I suppose it is the hind feet that make the front marks in the pattern. Rat, and possibly stoat and weasel, tracks will also be seen. Of birds, besides the small hopping birds one may observe the stride of a running pheasant, the footmarks of wood-pigeons, and perhaps a woodcock; this last is a very compact and neat track, as if the bird had taken the greatest pains to put one foot exactly in front of the other at each step. Near the burn footprints may be found that suggest a larger bird than any of these, and yet may be only those of a modest moorhen. So the countryman may walk about woods and fields, reading the snow as an archæologist reads the hieroglyphs on an ancient tablet. If frost continues, the hunger note of blackbirds searching for food, in open drains or wherever there is a sign of bare ground, becomes well known. In front of the garden door a space is cleared from snow and scraps of all sorts put out from time to time: here birds congregate and feed and squabble, particularly blackbirds: hunger does make them congregate where there is food, but does not make them merciful to each other. A hard winter is one of nature's opportunities to apply the principle of selection of the strongest and most resourceful for survival.

A perplexing problem confronts the feeder of birds if starlings discover his bounty. Starlings may come in great numbers, and they do not waste so much time as blackbirds in quarrelling and chasing each other; feeding in a flock is their habit; they descend upon the food; no other bird can get into that close crowd; they are active and intensely busy, and in a few minutes there is no food left. If rooks come, the situation is still worse. It is the garden birds and not these outsiders that we wish to feed, and, with all goodwill to starlings and rooks, it is not part of our plan to feed these strangers and let our garden birds be starved. There is no way of solving this problem which is not harsh or painful, and everyone must decide for himself how to attempt to deal with it.

Deep snow is an exception on low ground in England, and just because it is an exception the incidents connected with it fix themselves on the memory of childhood and remain with us. We remember the hard winters and forget the mild ones that made no impression upon us. So as we look back on past years we think of the exceptions as if they had been the rule, and we are apt to say that the climate has changed. 'I remember when I was a boy the roads were blocked and we drove between walls of snow, through lanes cut in the drifts': this is the sort of thing that is often said. Yes: this happened at home in my youth, but only twice in thirty years. It has happened once in the last thirty years. No general inference can be drawn from this. The frost that set in during January 1895 and lasted into March must have been as hard as the great frost of over a hundred years ago, when an ox was roasted whole upon the Thames. Once or twice only in a century is there such a frost in England, and it is remembered and quoted to younger generations in mild winters as evidence that the climate has changed. I doubt whether it has changed in living memory, or in recent times. When it is said that our winters are not so severe as they used to be, I am disposed to say, 'No, and they never were.'

It is also the fashion to say that our springs are colder than they used to be. I doubt also the truth of

this. March is called a spring month, and therefore
expected to be warm. Statistics do not warrant the
expectation. The first part of March is normally colder
than the first part of December. The average mean
temperature for the day on the 15th December is 40·8
degrees; the figure for the 10th March is only 40·9
degrees. These figures are stated to be founded upon
observations of sixty years, and reference to them
prevents surprise at cold in March or mildness in
December.

An exceptionally cold spring is, however, more
disastrous to birds than a hard winter. The succession
of blizzards that began in February 1917 and lasted
into April did more harm to birds than any weather
that I remember. Expert observers in some parts of
the country estimated that 70 per cent. of the song
thrushes perished, and long-tailed tits were scarce for
a few years afterwards. But as a rule our winters are
mild, and the birds that visit us or stay with us get
through the season without much distress.

Chapter VIII

Courtship, Mating and Family Life

British birds are monogamous; this is the rule, and the exceptions are few. I can think only of four: the cuckoo, ruffs and reeves, black game and capercaillie. Of these, cuckoos and ruffs and reeves are said to be polyandrous; the other two species are polygamous. All four are considered native British birds, though ruffs and reeves have ceased to breed in this Island, and it is said that the capercaillie had once died out and was reintroduced. Pheasants were not indigenous, this is also true of the ancestors of our poultry. These birds, therefore, need not be taken into account; the inferiority of their habits is not native to Britain, and our country is not responsible for them.

Some of the larger birds are believed to pair for life. This is asserted of wild geese and swans. I accept the statement, though I do not know how it has been proved by observation of birds in a wild state, especially of birds that are migratory. Mute swans, however, afford strong presumptive evidence of the truth of the statement. These birds are not native; they were introduced many centuries ago, and have remained domesticated; but they have also distributed themselves over the country, and many pairs live and breed in a perfectly natural state. They may be found in wild parts of the Highlands and islands of Scotland, and even there they seem to continue to be tame. I have seen them in wild surroundings, where they had established themselves, as tame as on ornamental water in a garden or park. They do therefore offer exceptional opportunities for observation under free conditions; and I imagine there is no doubt that a pair once mated never separate in life.

The habits of tame birds can only be offered tentatively as presumptive, and not positive evidence of habits of birds in a wild state; but with this reservation it may be relevant to quote a pair of Chiloe wigeon. They were reared by pinioned birds on the ponds at Fallodon, but have never themselves been under restraint. Owing to the kind forbearance of neighbours they have escaped being shot and are now in their fifth year. They are often absent, sometimes for a few weeks, but they come to the home ponds at every season of the year, and when there they are never seen apart; they are generally close together and seldom at a distance of two yards one from the other. They are closely mated throughout the year, and apparently for life. Being a foreign species, their choice of mates is limited; but some birds of their own kind are reared almost every year, and left at liberty; so that they are not absolutely without alternative choice. Generally speaking, it seems at least probable that swans, geese, sheldrakes and those kinds of waterfowl in which the plumage of the male and female is the same throughout the year, do pair for life in a wild state. In all these species there is probably no separation of the male from the female during the rearing of the young, and when this is so, there is no reason why the mating should not be permanent. It seems probable, also, that such birds as partridges and long-tailed tits, which have a prolonged time of family life, do mate permanently. Most of the small birds, however, seem to separate in the summer moult, and the pairs are completely broken. Chaffinches are an obvious example of this. Close observers say that the male warblers arrive in spring before the females; if this be so, there has undoubtedly been a separation between birds that nested in the preceding year. There will, however, be a tendency for each bird, male or female, to return to the same nesting place. In this way one pair of birds may meet there year after year, and mate again and again. This leads to pretty thoughts; we may imagine a hen blackcap, after months of separation, directing her journey from Africa to the familiar nesting place in England, and hearing, as she approaches, the same mate singing as he waits for her in the old territory; but as far as my observations have gone, this remains only pleasant speculation.

The birds that mate for life and remain together throughout the year evidently get a high degree of satisfaction from each other's company: this is much more than the pleasure that brings them together in the nesting season for the purpose of reproducing their species; and which is innate in living creatures, that they may be nature's instruments for maintaining and multiplying their kind. All birds have this, and some, as for instance the pheasant, may have little more than this. But others have much more. Birds that remain in pairs throughout the year are distressed if they are separated at any season, and to anyone who observes this and who watches them together, it is apparent that even in autumn and winter the mated birds have positive enjoyment in each other's society. Anyone who has watched tame waterfowl will know that, if the mate of one pair is taken away, it does not follow that the one which remains will take readily to the first new mate that is provided. An extreme example of this is the conduct of a red-crested pochard which is described in *Fallodon Papers*. Other instances could be given, but to cite them would involve the narrative in such minute detail as to make it tedious in the telling.

It can be said, therefore, that in many birds there is more than the impulse which brings males and females together in the nesting season: there is a special attachment of individual birds to each other. Individual selection is no doubt prompted by the general impulse of sex attraction, but sometimes it goes beyond or transcends it.

In most, and probably in all species of birds, there is some kind of 'display' by the male in courtship. In males that have no marked change of plumage this display is shown by unusual movements and attitudes. A very interesting description of this kind of display in courtship is given in *The British Warblers*, by Eliot Howard. Many male birds, however, have special plumage for the season of courtship; this is sometimes of an extraordinary character and seems to exist for the purpose of display. It is most remarkable in some foreign species, and in some instances must be an inconvenience to the bird for all purposes in life except that of display. The peacock is the illustration best known in Britain. A description of the courting attitudes of British waterfowl will be found in J. G. Millais's fine volumes on the British Diving and Surface-feeding Ducks. I shall not attempt to describe what is indescribable except by illustrations which are given in such books as these; but some comment is suggested by watching the birds in life.

It is assumed that their object is to impress the females, and there is no doubt some truth in this. Female teal, sometimes a single bird, may be watched inciting several males to display, and the performance may be continued for some time, the males whistling and displaying against each other, but not necessarily engaging in combat. If they slacken in their display the female will by voice and gesture give fresh incitement, and she evidently enjoys the performance. On the other hand, the astounding display of the peacock seems to impress human spectators much more than the attendant peahens, who often appear to be quite unconcerned. Indeed, sometimes in the season of courtship it seems to be the males of monogamous birds that admire the appearance of the female, and not the reverse. I have seen the sober-coloured female wood-duck standing on a stone a few inches above the surface, while the male bird, a most brilliant creature, sat in the water looking up at her, his bill opening and shutting as if in adoration of this wonderful mate, while the female appeared to take it all as a matter of course. I have never seen the male on the stone and the female in the water below admiring him. As the season of courtship advances, the female of this species and of others, as I have been able to

observe, is the dominant personality; it is she who
decides the movements of the day, the brilliant male
attending her, not exercising any influence upon the
direction she takes. Some time is spent in the early
spring wandering about in search of a nesting place,
and it is presumably the prerogative of the female to
choose it. The male bird recognises this as the main
business in hand, and follows, attentive but subservient. On the whole, I think it is not very profitable
to press the search for a utilitarian purpose too far in
the matter of brilliant plumage and display. The species
of birds in which the males have brilliant plumage do
not appear to thrive better than those in which the
males are as sober as the females. Each species of
bird has its own peculiar method of display; some are
slight, some quaint, some ludicrous, some amazing;
but we cannot suppose that each difference has a
utilitarian reason. The cock pheasant claps his wings
very audibly after he crows; the barn-door cock does
this before he crows. The little difference of habit
cannot be supposed to matter to the welfare of each
species. As with small differences, so it may be with
greater. It seems to me that wide differences in habits
of courtship and plumage serve little purpose, except
that of infinite variety, and that to press the utilitarian
theory very far is more likely to deviate into error
than to discover truth. I prefer to suppose that there
is in nature an aesthetic design which is a part of the

general purpose, and that the infinite variety of natural beauty is a manifestation of this.

Reserving till later the fascinating subject of nests and eggs, let us consider the family life of birds after the young leave the nest.

Rooks live in a community. I have not had the good fortune to be intimate with a rookery, and cannot therefore contribute anything of value on the life of rooks; but anyone who studied closely the life of a single rookery would provide himself with material for a whole book on this one subject. Rooks are monogamous, as anyone can see at nesting-time; what separate family life they have within the community after the young are fledged, or whether they pair for life, I do not know; but their community life seems to be permanent.

Our other common birds vary in their degree of family life. First come birds like the partridge and the long-tailed tit. In these species the young keep together and remain with the parents till the following spring: then it is time for them to break up into separate pairs; but till then, unless adverse circumstances break it up, the family remains together. Coveys of partridges may be broken up by shooting, and unattached birds may be admitted to a family to which they do not belong; but I believe the statement that each family endeavours to keep together is generally true. One or two families of long-tailed tits may amalgamate, for twenty or thirty birds are sometimes seen in one flock in the winter; but flocks of about twelve are common, and these I take to be one family. They are said to sleep touching each other in a row, perched on a branch. In the daytime they are constantly on the move, drifting through the woods, each bird flitting independently, but all keeping up a call note, or rather notes, for they have two that are very distinct. The purpose of this habit is no doubt to keep the family together.

Goldfinches appear to have more than the average family life of birds akin to them. Little parties of about six birds may be seen together in the autumn, and I imagine these to be each a family that has remained united. A 'charm' of goldfinches was the old expression for these little parties.

The general rule, however, for our common birds is to have as little family life with their young as is compatible with maintaining their kind. The young birds, when they have learnt to feed themselves, either drift or are driven away. In some instances – the robin may be one of these – the affection of the parent birds changes rapidly into animosity towards their young; in others the change is only to indifference: the result is the same, the family is dispersed.

One habit which I have noticed only with the moorhen, or merehen, as it should more appropriately be called, may be worth recording. Perhaps it is well known, but I have seen it only in the moorhen, and have not come across it in accounts of other species; it shall therefore be given in some detail.

A pair of moorhens nest every year on a pond in the garden. One May, about the middle of the month, they had hatched their brood, and, as usual, picked up bread thrown to them and fed the young with it; so far there was nothing remarkable; but about the middle of July, when a second brood was hatched, the young ones of May still remained with the parents and assisted in the feeding of the July brood. There were three survivors of the May brood: they were now full-feathered and independent, but still young birds easily to be distinguished from the old ones. A parent bird would pick up bread, put it into the beak of one of the May young, which would in turn feed one of the tiny July young. The process was repeated again and again, and was a matter of amusement to us for several days. There were also diverting variations in the procedure. Once a May young one, having received a piece of bread from a parent, transferred it to the beak of another May bird, which then fed one of the little July birds with it. In this manner the July brood were fed at second- or third-hand. Apparently it was against the rules for them to receive bread from a parent at first-hand, for, when a parent bird did for once put bread straight into the beak of a July bird, one of the May birds at once ran up, took the bread

out of the beak of the infant bird, and then replaced
it there. 'Sheer red tape' was the comment of one to
whom the story was related. The incidents described
took place on the garden path within a few yards of
my brother and myself, so that every detail could be
seen. Another year a young moorhen of a first brood
constantly took bread thrown to it and fed a young
one of a second brood; in this instance the performance was in the water. In all these instances the
moorhens were birds that had come to the pond by
their own choice and were in a natural state.

It is said that unmated or bereaved old birds of
various species sometimes join in the feeding of young
birds that do not belong to them; but as far as my
observations go, the example given by moorhens of
this early development in young birds of a desire to
undertake family duties is exceptional.

John Stuart Mill began at a very early age to teach
a younger brother and sister, but he did not do this
voluntarily, and he tells us that he greatly disliked
doing it. The conduct of the young moorhens was
voluntary and apparently agreeable to themselves.

Moorhens have a prolonged breeding season: on
this same pond there were newly hatched birds this
year in the week of the 22nd–29th August; but when
the breeding season is over, the conduct of the old
birds to the young ones is as harsh as that of old
birds of many other species.

Moorhens are in more than one respect odd birds; they will frequent a garden, where they are constantly confronted with mankind, without ever gaining confidence. If they are feeding on the lawn the appearance of a gardener will cause as much alarm and as quick a rush for refuge as if they were in imminent danger: other birds that were so very shy would either become more confident or leave the place.[1] If disturbed suddenly in the water, they often dive and come up amongst sedge or other cover, keeping the whole body submerged and exposing only the tip of the beak for breath. They seem to have a particular dislike to the jar of alighting on hard ground, and in flying across even a narrow strip of water will generally alight in the water and thence walk out; for a short flight they leave the legs dangling, but if they make up their minds to tuck up their legs they can fly very well and at some height. A moorhen is not entirely a ground and water bird, and is often found unexpectedly high up in a thick bush, such as laurel.

As an example of parental care for the young by partridges, the following incident may be given:

A pair of old birds with their young were dusting in an open road on the Hampshire downs; as I

---

[1] The moorhens spoken of here, though comparatively tame, have responded less to the great pains taken with birds than any of the waterfowl. Wild wigeon, pintail, etc., if they stay at all, become more tame than any of the moorhens that are always about the pond.

approached on a bicycle they ran behind a straggling thicket of thorn and bramble. I dismounted, left the bicycle and went round the bushes after the covey to get a nearer sight of them. They were used to people passing along the road, and, not expecting to be followed, had stopped a few yards off on the edge of a large bramble patch. I came quietly and suddenly upon them; the young were in down, without a feather; flying was out of the question for them, and the covey disappeared at once into the impenetrable brambles – all but two of the little birds: these adopted the alternative concealment of squatting on the open grass. I stood still, with these two birds at my feet, and waited to see what the next move would be. There were slight movements in the brambles, and little sounds that suggested consultation between the old birds. The little birds outside remained motionless. After a few minutes one of the old birds, with great fuss and éclat, burst out of the brambles three or four yards in front of me, and invited pursuit by the usual manœuvre of pretending to make frantic efforts to escape and to be unable to fly. My intention being to keep my eyes on the little birds at my feet, I did not stir limb or head; but so sudden and noisy was the old partridge's burst from the bush, that for one instant my gaze was diverted; in that one instant the two little birds at my feet disappeared: they were gone without my seeing them go: all was quiet in the brambles, nothing to be seen or heard of the covey except the single parent trying to decoy me away. Their manoeuvres were crowned with success by my withdrawing.

We can interpret these proceedings as we will. One suggestion is that the parent birds were aware that two of the brood were left outside, unsheltered and apparently in imminent danger; the sounds heard in the bush were instructions for them on no account to move. The action of one parent bird was part of a concerted plan to draw off my attention, and at the chosen moment the little birds at my feet received an order from the bush to bolt inside it. When once they had joined the others there was nothing more to be done, and all was quiet and silent in the brambles. This interpretation is not so very fanciful. Anyone who has observed young birds in a nest or on the ground must have seen how instantly they will obey the warning note of a parent bird to crouch and be still, and thus remain until further instructed.

A more prosaic interpretation of the whole affair is that the parent birds did not even know that two of the young had been left outside; the little birds squatted because it is one of the ways by which their kind conceal themselves. The shock of the outburst of the old bird frightened them, and they ran for shelter. The manœuvre of the old bird had no reference to the little birds outside, but was the usual device to relieve the covey generally of the inconvenience of my presence; and the silence in the bush was in order that the old bird outside might have the whole of my attention. However this may be, the fact remains that my deliberate object had been to keep my eyes on the two young birds at my feet, and that this was completely defeated.

Chapter IX

Nests and Eggs

Eggs are fragile things. It is therefore necessary for birds to place them where they will be protected from accidents: eggs are also greatly desired by ground vermin and by some kinds of predatory birds; it is therefore necessary for birds to endeavour to conceal their eggs. The shell, judging from the substance of which it is made, would naturally be white; in some cases it is so, but in others there is an infinite variety of colour. It would be reasonable to suppose that this variety of colour has been evolved to help in concealing the egg. That protective colouration exists in some insects is an irresistible conclusion: why should this theory not apply to the colouring of eggs of birds? We notice that some birds build in holes, where the eggs are not exposed to view; there is no need to protect these by colouration, and the eggs of woodpeckers, that nest in holes of trees, are white. The stock-dove also nests in holes of trees or ivy tods, or some very thick place where the nest is concealed from view, and its eggs are white. We are therefore easily started on the theory that the colouring of eggs is protective, but we soon get into difficulties. The wood-pigeon's nest is fairly open to view, and the eggs on it are so exposed as to be conspicuous. We should therefore expect protective colour to occur here; but wood-pigeons' eggs are pure white. It must be admitted that the wood-pigeons multiply in spite of the whiteness of their eggs, and that protective colour is therefore not needed to preserve the species; but I think their eggs leave the protective colouring theory something to answer; and there are other questions to follow. Rooks' eggs need protection less than wood-pigeons'; the nests and eggs are equally exposed, but the community of rooks is a defence against marauding crows, jackdaws or other egg-raiding birds, and each pair of rooks is much more able to ward of such raiders than a pair of defenceless wood-pigeons – *imbelles columbae*. Why has nature taken the trouble to give rooks' eggs colour, while withholding it from wood-pigeons, which seem to be more in need of it? This suggests caprice in the working of the protective theory.

Reflection will suggest other awkward questions. Why should a redstart and a dunnock both have eggs coloured blue, when the eggs of one of these birds are concealed in a hole and those of the other laid in an open nest? And can the blue eggs of the dunnock, a purer and brighter blue than those of the redstart, be any protection when seen against the dark lining of the open nest?

On the other hand, the eggs of many ground-nesting birds have colouring that must be protective: this is so with birds that breed on shingle. I have seen the nest of a Thick-knee on a down, where there were many molehills and stray chalk-flints of various shapes and sizes: the eggs of the Thick-knee looked very like chalk-flints that had been in contact with molehills. Think, too, how the gathering of plovers' eggs would be made easy if they were white, instead of being coloured as they are.

Now let us consider guillemots' eggs. The birds lay the eggs on bare ledges of rock and breed in colonies or crowds. The breeding place is so open and notorious that every marauding gull must know the eggs are there. It is the dense mass of guillemots that protects their eggs: for the purpose of protection the colour of the eggs can be of no use: yet nature has taken pains to make guillemots' eggs very curious, elaborate

and varied in colour and markings. The great danger
to which each guillemot's egg is exposed is that of
rolling off the bare ledge on which it is laid; there is
continual hustling and jostling in the crowd, as individual birds go and return. Against this danger the
eggs are protected by shape; the small end is exceptionally small in comparison with the large end. The
egg therefore, when disturbed, rolls round in one spot,
from which, unless absolutely pushed in one direction,
it will not roll away. The conclusion of the matter is
that in many, if not in the majority of birds, the
colouring of eggs has no protective value. If this was
so originally, it is so no longer, and it is only in some,
not in all birds that the colour of their eggs serves
this purpose.

Some classes of birds lay coloured eggs that have
no markings. Swans, geese and ducks are an example
of this: the eggs of one species may differ from those
of another in colour, but they are all plain.

The eggs of tits are white with red spots, and there
is a tendency for birds of the same family to have a
similar plan of colour. The eggs of buntings appear
to be marked with some kind of mysterious script, so
curious are the lines upon them: the eggs of the reed-
bunting look as if the script had been badly blotted:
they are astonishing and suggest an egg in a nightmare.
There is much in which I can see only caprice in the
colour and marking of eggs: dunnocks, starlings and

redstarts lay eggs of beautiful colour, but plain, without markings; in other birds we find all varieties of spots, blotches and mottling. One or two species have the misfortune to be variable in the colour of their eggs: clutch after clutch is then taken by egg collectors that they may have examples of every type of egg of this one species represented in their collection. The tree pipit suffers from this misfortune, and it is said that the number of clutches of tree pipits' eggs to be found in a single collection is sometimes infamous.

The red-backed shrike is reported to suffer in the same way, but the only eggs I have found of this bird have been of one type. It is a curious type: the ends of the egg are without markings, but a zone or girdle of thick-set spots goes round the egg not far from the larger end.

Our small birds hatch their eggs in about fourteen days or a little less, and another period of about the same time is needed before the young leave the nest: when first hatched they are naked and helpless. This is the rule with birds whose young do not leave the nest till they can fly: the larger the bird the longer is the time needed to hatch the eggs and rear the young to independence.

Some birds have an entirely different plan of reproduction. The eggs do not hatch till the young are covered with down and able to run. Young waterfowl leave the nest with their parent as soon as the hatching is complete, and they are able at once to swim and dive and get their own food. It is most entertaining to watch an infant brood of pochards or tufted ducks diving for natural food. On the other hand, young moorhens, which when hatched leave the nest as capable as little ducks of swimming and diving, are piteously incapable of feeding themselves, and for many days depend on their parents to find and put food into their beaks.

Young partridges are, when hatched, able to run and get their own food, but they and other land birds of this kind have a difference from little ducks. Young ducks do not get the power of flight till they are approaching the size of adult birds: young partridges, on the other hand, grow feathers and can fly short distances even when still quite small. Young ducks can protect themselves from ground vermin by a rush into water: young partridges cannot do this, and nature has given them the compensation of being able to fly at an early stage.

The rule is not absolute that birds nest on the ground if their young are able to leave the nest as soon as the eggs hatch.[1] The mallard, our common wild duck, sometimes makes a nest above the ground. I have seen one on a horizontal oak branch clothed

---

1 Of course numbers of birds, whose young cannot leave the nest when hatched, also nest on the ground.

with ivy at a height of seven feet. Mandarin and wood-ducks habitually nest in holes in trees: an instance of newly hatched wood-ducks safely descending unaided from a height of twenty-one feet is related in *Fallodon Papers*.

The strength possessed by young ducks when they emerge from the egg is remarkable. I have known a brood of young mandarins travel with their mother a distance of 350 yards through long grass. The nest was visited in the morning, and the duck was then sitting on it. In the afternoon the young birds, about nine in number, all arrived at the water showing no signs of exhaustion.

Young moorhens are equally vigorous. I once disturbed a moorhen from her nest when the eggs were on the point of hatching: they were at my feet, apparently intact. There was a loud cheeping of young moorhens, which I did not at first connect with this nest. For some time I looked about for a brood, surprised that there should be another family so close, for moorhens are pugnacious birds in the breeding season. The noise continued, and at length I found that it proceeded from the eggs. On examination, I found they were chipping; the beaks of some of the young birds were exposed, and from these came as much sound as if the brood were already launched in the water and had begun their open-air life.

Eggs are interesting, curious, and often beautiful;

but more wonderful are nests. I suppose it must be said that birds choose a site and build a nest by instinct and not by intelligence; for each bird that builds a nest for the first time does this after the manner of its kind, without teaching or experience to bring the faculty of reason into action.

Instinct, then, must have the credit of what is done, but the result is wonderful. Some birds, such as the guillemot, make no nest at all, and some birds, such as the nightjar, as well as some that nest on shingle, make no nest unless it be a mere scoop. But the skill of some nest-building birds is extraordinary: admirable is a fit epithet, for the skill deserves both praise and wonder. With nests, as with plumage, we find differences so great that they seem to be manifesting nature's love of infinite variety.

The subject of nests alone would fill a whole volume, if it were to be dealt with by someone who had given close study to it. Only a few outstanding features that have caught my own attention can be dealt with here.

The most elaborate nest of our common birds, the one on which the greatest care and labour are expended, is that of the long-tailed tit.

A description of the nest, the method and actions of the birds in building it, and a detailed account of one particular nest that I had an opportunity of observing from time to time till the birds fledged, has

been given elsewhere.[1] This need not be repeated
here; but a description of the actual fledging of the
birds which I had the privilege of observing may be
of some interest. The nest had been found in an early
stage of construction on the first Sunday in March.
On the morning of the 19th May I was standing near
it, watching the parent birds arriving with food for
the young. A large lime tree projected over the end
of the sweetbriar hedge in which the nest was. From
this direction the parent birds kept arriving with food,
advancing along the top of the hedge, uttering a note
as they came. There was commotion in the nest
whenever the approach of a parent was heard, and a
struggle from within to get a head to the opening.
Presently in this repeated struggle one eager little bird
seemed to be thrust out by the pressure behind: as
the parents kept returning with food this process went
on. When the first bird had gone out, competition to
meet the approaching parents soon emptied the nest;
the young birds advanced continually along the hedge
in the direction from which the old birds came, and
in no long time the whole family were up in the lime
tree in the full activity of free life. It appears that
young birds reared in a nest such as this, or in a hole
of some depth from which egress is difficult, remain
longer in the nest, and are therefore more active and

1 *Fallodon Papers* ('Pleasure in Nature').

strong when they first leave it than birds that flop over the edge of an open nest. Long-tailed tits are remarkably various in their choice of a site. With most birds, we know to within a few feet the height at which the nest will be found and the kind of place it will occupy. Long-tailed tits have two very different types of place. They sometimes nest in a bush, especially a bush such as whin, juniper or *Rosa rugosa*. Here the nest will be only three, four or five feet above the ground, and with no more solid support than the twigs of the bush afford. Sometimes the site chosen is the sturdy fork of an oak or ash. In such a place the nest is solidly supported beneath and buttressed by a stout stem on each side. These nests are, in my experience, often high up, and it would need a fairly long ladder to reach them. They are well concealed from eyes below, for they look like a mere thickening of the fork of the tree.

March is the time for finding the nests of the long-tailed tits. The little rattle, which is their most distinctive note, is very frequently uttered and calls attention to the bird. Field glasses will show whether they have any nesting material in their beaks: if this is so, a very short observation will see the bird go to where the nest is being built. The morning hours before midday are the business time for nest building, and with a little care and patience every long-tailed tit's nest in the neighbourhood can be found; according to my observation, the time occupied from the first beginning of the nest to the day when the young leave it is about eleven weeks. This must be nearly or quite double the corresponding period for most little woodland birds. Others more fortunate than myself can say how long it generally takes a pair of these birds to complete a nest; but some notion of the labour and time expended may be formed by considering the number of feathers used in the lining. A friend of mine counted 1660 separate feathers out of one nest that had been built in his garden; and *British Birds* quotes 1776 as having been found in one nest. At my sister's house in Hampshire a long-tailed tit, at this stage of its nest building, was seen to alight on the back of a white turkey cock and pluck a feather from that huge living store. As the nest is a bag with only one small opening near but not at the top, the heat and stuffiness inside must be intense. It is surprising that some of the young birds are not stifled; but I have not found evidence of mortality inside a nest, and the usual size of a family of long-tailed tits proves that the percentage of birds fledged to eggs laid is very good. This is on the assumption that the nest is not destroyed. Eleven weeks is a long time for such a nest to escape every malevolent eye. Nor is it only desire to eat eggs or young that may bring an enemy: the warm, soft material of the nest may be coveted. I had found a long-tailed tit's nest in a small yew tree at Fallodon in the Easter recess: at Whitsuntide I looked for it in vain; there was no trace of it in the yew tree: in an adjoining yew tree was a squirrel's drey, and to this the whole of the tit's nest had been ruthlessly transferred and there used as a lining. Much space has been given to this one small species, but it is not easy to part from the subject of long-tailed tits, their nests and little ways.

The varieties and peculiarities of nests and of sites chosen for them are very great. Sometimes the reason for the peculiarity is apparent. For instance, the cup of the reed-warbler's nest is unusually deep: the nest is woven on to the stems of the reeds and is tilted when the reeds are swayed in a strong wind: the depth of the cup lessens the risk of the eggs being rolled out of the nest. Here there is a reason for the peculiarity of the reed-warbler's nest satisfactory to our intelligence; but many variations in nest building provoke questions that leave us puzzled and silent. Some warblers line their nests profusely with feathers, and the whole structure is designed for warmth: but the blackcap and garden-warbler get on very well with the thinnest possible open nest, with no warm lining. So thin is a blackcap's nest that the eggs can sometimes be seen through the bottom of the nest by one looking up from below. Anyone who sleeps out of doors knows how important it is to have protection below as well as above; but the blackcap's nest is not constructed to keep in the warmth of the bird's body: ventilation and not warmth seems to be the object. The blackcap is an example of great economy in the use of material; it is a wonder that out of such little material a cup can be built that will hold eggs at all. If the long-tailed tit is to be admired for showing how elaborate a nest can be, the blackcap must be credited with excellent skill in making the most of very little material.

Willow-warblers, chiff-chaffs and wood-warblers all build domed nests with a large opening on one side. Two of these species nest on the ground,[1] the chiff-chaff in some thick bush a foot or two above the ground. The willow-warbler and the chiff-chaff line their nests profusely with feathers; the wood-warbler does without them. Is there some subtle difference in the physique of these kindred birds that makes feathers in the nest essential to two of them and indifferent to the third? Or is the use of feathers by the willow-warbler and chiff-chaff sheer luxury?

Variations in nests and the questions that they provoke are innumerable; but only a few more points that have seemed to me specially pleasant or interesting can be mentioned.

---

1 Like all general statements, there are exceptions to this. A willow-warbler once nested about two feet up in the trellis on the cottage: there was no connection of herbage or plant growth between the nest and the ground.

Every chaffinch's nest is a delight on account of its neatness: indeed each one seems neater than our recollection of previous nests. As described in an earlier chapter, there is a touch of commonplace about the bird and its ways, but there is real distinction and refinement in the nest: it surpasses all other nests that I know in neatness. I have never seen the cock chaffinch take any part in building the nest or in sitting on the eggs. One interesting experience of the resourcefulness of a hen chaffinch came under my notice. The bird had nested in the creepers on the cottage: it had been sitting for a few days on three eggs; one morning the nest was empty: some animal or bird had robbed it. Later in the day a hen chaffinch was flying industriously to and fro between the cottage and a place in a hedge some twenty yards away. The repeated flights invited closer attention; the bird was engaged in removing the empty nest piecemeal and reconstructing it in the hedge. Business in London prevented me from noting how many days were occupied in completing the nest in the hedge, or whether any new materials were used for it: but all the material of the nest on the cottage was removed, and the bird again sat on three eggs in the recon-structed nest: it is curious that the clutch should have been so small in the first as well as in the second laying. Unhappily the eggs were again taken by some marauder and this time the nest remained empty and abandoned. There was no sign by which to identify the mate of this hen chaffinch: he took no part in these proceedings. He was presumably one of two or three cock chaffinches that were within hearing of the place, and probably continued to sing with undiminished spirit.

All sorts of places provide nesting sites for birds: some nest underground in a hole; others in holes in trees; others nest on the ground, whether it be on bare earth, shingle or rock, or in grass or heather; others nest in bushes or trees; and some, such as swifts, swallows, and house-martins, have become dependent on the buildings of mankind. As a rule, birds desire some support under the nest, whether this be firm ground, or twigs or branches or some ledge or rafter; but three common exceptions occur to me. The peculiarity of the reed-warbler's nest has already been noticed; the house-martin's nest, which is firmly attached to the top and side of some corner in a building, but has no underneath support, is familiar to everybody; the third exception is the nest of the gold-crest. This does not rest on a branch, but is slung underneath it. An evergreen tree, such as a silver fir, is generally used; the tiny cup of the nest is admirably concealed by the thick-set green spines of the fir branch above it.

One particular nest of a kingfisher may be described for the sake of its attractive secrecy. A small side

stream of the Itchen ran for some distance entirely
concealed by trees at the edge of beautiful pleasure
grounds, Yews, chestnuts and other large trees stood
thick together on one side of it; on the other side
were willows; the canopy of boughs hid the stream,
and it was known to us as 'the hidden brook.' A
willow tree was blown down and lay prone on the
water-meadow: a great block of bank was lifted and
held upright by the roots of the tree: so high was this
and so far over did the boughs spread from trees on
the other side, that the gap left by the fallen willow
did not expose the stream or disturb its privacy. Into
this lifted bank kingfishers had tunnelled from the
inner side. By going in among the trees the hole could
be seen, but could not be reached even on its own
side without wading in the water. Here a pair of
kingfishers nested every year, flying up and down the
green tunnel in which the stream ran, and going to
and from their nest unseen. In course of time the
earth began to wear away. On the outer side between
two of what had been surface roots there came to be
a little opening. By putting an eye to this the eggs
could be seen; and by inserting a small twig I once
extracted an egg. I was thus in possession of a
kingfisher's egg that had been obtained without disturbing the nest – a rare privilege, for, as a rule, I
suppose a kingfisher's egg can only be obtained by
digging out the nest. The kingfisher's eggs are called

white: correctly, no doubt, but they have a delicate tinge of colour, due to the yolk showing through the white shell, which is unusually transparent. I do not remember that there was any horrible smell about this nest, but the dark slimy-looking stuff that oozed out of the entrance used by the birds suggested foulness within the passage, if not in the nest itself.

For a few years after this nest was first found, it was matter of importance to be sure that the birds nested successfully there each season; but gradually the weather and the natural processes of decay wore away the earth, till it became a mere skeleton of decaying roots, and no one who had not seen it as it had once been could have imagined that it could ever have been a kingfisher's breeding place.

To say that nests may be underground, on the ground, in or on houses, in bushes or in trees, is a fairly comprehensive statement; but it is not complete. Some nests of grebes may be said to be in the water. The little grebe or dabchick's nest is a blob of dark, dank, sodden weed: it is often placed in a bed of weed in the middle of a chalk-stream, where the bird when sitting is in full view. But the sitting bird also has a clear view, and whenever a suspicious object approaches the grebe covers its eggs and goes off, so that the nest appears only as an uninteresting patch of dead weed. This ruse of the dabchick is a sight very familiar to chalk-stream anglers; as the angler crosses the fence to enter a water-meadow he may see a dabchick rise up on a patch of weeds in the river, hurriedly pull weed over its eggs, then dive with the least possible movement, and so slip away unseen to some concealment. The bird will do this when the angler is still 50 or 100 yards away. The habit of most birds is to sit motionless and tight on a nest; the nearer it is approached the closer will the bird sit: it will not move till in imminent danger of capture or even till actually evicted by touch. This is an example of endeavour to escape notice by the concealment of stillness. The dabchick is an example of the alternative method; that of leaving before a possible enemy has come near enough to see that there is a nest. I have known a spotted flycatcher practise this method when sitting on eggs. One that used to nest on the Hampshire cottage would fly off the nest in a light unconcerned manner whenever a human head appeared round the corner. Chaffinches, on the other hand, would sit very close, and if put off the nest would leave it with fluster and distress.

That dabchicks can fly is proved by their temporary appearance at migratory seasons of the year in unwonted places, to which they can only have come by flying; but diving is their usual method of movement. When the object is to escape, the dabchick dives with the least possible mark on the surface of the water. I have had one singular experience to the contrary. I was kneeling on the bank of the Itchen and putting my fly to a rising trout. My knees were at the water's edge: I bent forward for the purpose of casting: my attention was concentrated on the spot where the trout was rising. I became aware that something was going on in the river close to me and that I was being sprinkled with drops of water. I looked down to discover what unusual thing was happening, saw a dabchick come to the surface close to me, and dive with as much splash and disturbance as possible, throwing up, as it did so, some drops of water that reached me; the bird repeated this exploit several times. In front of me in the thin strip of sedge that grew in the water was the dark blob of the nest; the unwonted conduct of the bird was a desperate attempt, if not to drown, at least to annoy and so get rid of me. I have read somewhere that a flock of coots, when threatened by a hawk, will all dive together, throwing up as much water as they can when the hawk stoops, as if in the hope of drowning it. No doubt my dabchick had the encouragement, when it returned to its nest, of thinking that its little efforts had saved the eggs from an impending monster.

One pretty way that the dabchick has with its young was shown me on the water in St James's Park. When I was first in office and kept in London from 1892–95, I made acquaintance with the man who then looked after the waterfowl, and who lived across the isthmus that is opposite the windows of the Foreign Office. At his cottage I used to call in the season to hear news of the breeding waterfowl, and he would show me various nests. One morning as he was taking me round the island he pointed out a dabchick's nest attached to some willow branches that hung into the water. When we came near he exclaimed that the eggs must have hatched since he had seen the nest earlier in the morning, for the nest was now empty. We heard a curious little noise on the water, and looking out beyond the branches saw the parent dabchick and her lately hatched young ones. Being suspicious of us, she had warned the young and now presented her body to them as they sat in the water. Instinct told them what was required: each bird got on to the back of the old one, and was there covered by her folded wings. When all the young had mounted, the parent swam away with her whole family, compact, concealed and safe.

I suppose that other grebes have similar habits as regards nests and young, but I have not had the opportunities of observing them closely. The dabchick does not attempt to rival other grebes in brightness of plumage. The great-crested grebe is the only one of these that I have seen in breeding plumage: the head of both sexes is then adorned with bright feathers, and these and the erect carriage of neck and head as they swim make the birds very distinguished. A pair of great crested grebes give distinction to any piece of water which they choose as a nesting place.

Birds sometimes make use of the empty nest of another species, or even use a nest of their own a second time. Two broods of blackbirds were reared in one season in one nest on the Hampshire cottage; whether this was done by one and the same bird or by two different birds I cannot be certain; I assumed it to be done by one bird. After the second brood of blackbirds had left this nest a pair of pied wagtails lined it with a new cup of their own making, and successfully hatched and reared a brood. Three successive broods were thus reared in this one nest in one season. I have known a spotted flycatcher put a new lining in the empty nest of a chaffinch and use this successfully for its own eggs and young.

In contrast to this tendency to save labour in nest building by using a ready-made nest, some birds build more nests than are ever used for their own eggs. The moorhen, for instance, makes several nests. In this case it seems as if the birds felt bound to do more than once what can be done so easily; for the moor-hen's nest is simple and easily constructed of material that lies ready about it. But the extra nests are not always superfluous: I have seen one used regularly for

the young birds. This nest had never had eggs in it; it
was near to and in full view of the place where I sat
to feed waterfowl after sunset. Every evening for
several days a parent moorhen conducted her young
family swimming to the nest; assembled them on it
and brooded them there.

Simple as a moorhen's nest appears, I have seen
a bird taking what appeared to be unnecessary
trouble about it. A moorhen was observed searching
the ground near one of the ponds at Fallodon and
selecting large dead leaves. These it conveyed to a
small clump of yellow iris growing in the water by
the bank. I assumed that the bird was building a
nest, and when it had apparently ceased working, I
examined the clump of iris. The nest was there,
but so also was the moorhen, sitting on a full
clutch of eggs. The bird had therefore been
improving the nest some time after the eggs had
been laid in it.

A more remarkable instance of prolific nest building
is that of the common wren. After the long-tailed tit's
nest, that of the wren is the most elaborate. In this
case there is no question of the bird making more
than one nest, simply because, as in the case of the
moorhen, nest building is easy. Yet one pair of wrens
will make several nests; each nest is constructed with
great care and perfect skill; but only the one that is
destined for eggs is lined with feathers. We can

therefore with certainty tell 'cock' nests from those that have contained eggs. The number of these empty 'cock' nests is a great disappointment to anyone who searches for nests in order to find eggs or young. If these 'cock' nests are visited after sunset in autumn and winter, they are often found to be used by a single bird as a bed-chamber; and sometimes in summer a stream of strong young wrens will issue from a 'cock' nest, showing that it is used as a resting or roosting place for a family.

Mr Burkitt has made particularly interesting and minute observation of this habit of a pair of wrens, and the following quotation is from a paper by him in *The Irish Naturalist*; it is reprinted here with his permission:

The male had a nest, C1, built in a low bush on the 17th April. On the 27th he had another, C2, nearly built in St John's-wort at the opposite end of his domain from C1, and 100 yards from it. On the 3rd May he was building another, C3, in ivy about midway between the first two. On the 10th May I found him (?) lodged in C2 at 9.30 P.M. On the 11th he was singing hard a yard from C3 and flying in and out. On the 15th and 17th he was still working at the latter. A bird was lodged in it at 10 P.M. on the 18th. The 19th May was the first time I got a sight of an apparent mate with this male, and near C3. The next day, the 20th, there were some feathers in C3, and at 10 P.M. on the 21st the female (?) was in it and one egg. On the 22nd I found the male was well on with another nest, C4, near C1, in an exposed sapling under the trees. The male when building his nest sings much, and seems to make unnecessary alarms, and it was this alarm which showed him to me as back again, going in and out of C2 on the 27th. On the 28th I saw him at C4. On the 30th and 31st he was at C2 alarming and singing, and staying inside for ten or fifteen minutes; and for a week later his singing and interest seemed to be at this end of his domain, separated from his sitting mate by my house and a wide open space. I may note here that I cannot find that any male helps to feed the brood as long as they are in the nest, or takes any interest whatever at that time. In four cases I have kept the feeding female out of the nest for a lengthened time, making her sound much alarm, without producing any sign whatever of the male. But in the only case C in which I watched the brood *after* being fledged, the male certainly did take a very distinct interest; whether it was more in the young or in the female I cannot say. I am not clear whether he then took part in the feeding.

On the evening of the day the young left the nest I found one of them perched in the entrance of C4, and observed curious excitement of both parents around this nest, which was explained two nights later by finding the four young lodged in it, the night being cold but dry. They had also been about C2, but I cannot say whether they lodged in it, or how often they lodged in C4. I did not like to interfere with the nests too much. C4 was a very suitable nest for lodgings as it was especially deep owing to its situation in a fork, but it was exposed to view beside a path.

The feeding of the young continued for at least a fortnight after they were fledged – till 13th July. I was thinking the female might start a second brood in C2 or C4, but I suppose the 13th July would be rather late to recommence. All singing of wrens stopped about the 18th July.

On 6th July, while fledged young were still being fed, the male (?) was visiting C2, and on the 11th I noticed this nest had been filled with moss to the entrance. The old breeding nest C3 I then found had its entrance also closed, but it was not filled up inside. C4 was not closed. C1 had been damaged for a considerable time and therefore did not play any part.

Some birds normally rear more than one brood in the year. As soon as the first brood is independent the female parent begins to lay a second clutch of eggs, generally in a new nest. It would be reasonable to suppose that such birds would in time become more numerous than birds that are content with rearing only one brood in a season. The chaffinch, however, which maintains its position as one of our most common and numerous birds, is single-brooded. It will make a second attempt if the first nest is destroyed, but its objective is to rear one brood of four or five young, and after this has been attained I have never seen chaffinches make a second effort. The number of any one species of our resident birds is decided mainly by adaptability to surroundings, by abundance or shortage of food supply, and by combat within the species itself to drive away superfluous birds, and thus prevent overcrowding.

The cirl-bunting in my experience diminished very much in numbers in the neighbourhood of the cottage, though it is a very pertinacious breeder, if the following instance is a guide to the habits of the species.

It was the early morning of the 27th June 1900. I was shaving in the little dressing room at the cottage when I became aware of a cock cirl-bunting sitting on a branch of a young acacia a few yards off in front of the window. His manner was uneasy and embarrassed. He evidently saw me and did not like me. If he objected to my presence he was free to go away: why, then, did he remain? The answer was clear enough: he wanted to do something, and he did not want me to see him doing it. The thing that birds most dislike is to be seen going to a nest: from the behaviour of the cirl-bunting it was evident that he had a nest and that it was near to me. I had not hitherto seen a cirl-bunting's nest: no doubt this one could be found now that I knew whereabout it must be; but it would be convenient if the bird would show me the exact place. To disarm suspicion I pretended not to see him and went on shaving. Before I had finished he had flown into a place in the thuja hedge about five yards from my window, remained there for some seconds, and then had flown out again. My note made at the time does not mention that I saw any food in his beak, but probably he was feeding young birds. I hurried to the spot and found the nest, with two very young birds and one addled egg. Till the 5th July all went well with the nest: between that date and the 7th some villain, probably a jackdaw, took the young birds. We were not at the cottage after the 10th July, and the further efforts of this pair of cirl-buntings were related to us by W. H. Hudson, to whom the cottage was lent for the rest of that summer. The birds made another nest in the sweetbriar hedge at the other side of the cottage, and this time successfully reared three young birds. Having accomplished this, the indefatigable pair made another nest in another part of the sweetbriar hedge: eggs were laid in this, but it was deserted: probably the hen bird felt that for one season she had done enough. After this there were high hopes that this little plot of home ground would be honoured with a cirl-bunting's nest every season; but it was not to be. There was no cirl-bunting's nest there in any subsequent year. Cirl-buntings, which had been plentiful in that region, became scarce; and for some years before my cottage times came to an end in 1922 I had not heard a cirl-bunting within earshot of the place. It is often so with anything specially interesting observed in nature: hopes are raised and then disappointed, or it may be the reverse: there is increase and decrease, ebb and flow, waxing and waning.[1]

It is a fascinating pursuit, when there is leisure for it, to look for the nests in the garden or neighbourhood of a country home. The discovery of a well-hidden nest with eggs gives a sense of delicate privilege; the watching of its subsequent welfare is a continuing interest; and if the end is happy and the young birds leave the nest safely, we feel deeply satisfied. Yet birds, if they could address us, might well say, 'However kindly your interest and however benevolent your intention, please do not look for our nests. You will expose them to dangers of which you do not dream and from which you cannot save them.' At the Hampshire cottage the destruction of nests in the little garden and the thickets of the adjoining chalk-pit was heart breaking. The nests that were known to be destroyed were, of course, nests that we had found and were watching: otherwise we should not have known of their fate. The proportion of those that came to grief was so large that in some years it seemed that the breeding season must be a

---

1 Some account of the first and second nesting of this pair of cirl-buntings, and also a description of the cottage and its surroundings, can be found in W. H. Hudson's *Hampshire Days*, chapters xii. and xiii.

failure. It never was so: there was always a good output of young birds from nests that we had not found. There was no reason to think that human mischief was to blame for the robbing of nests in this particular spot. There were stoats, weasels, rats, field mice and jackdaws, and these were enough to account for all the damage: but why did the particular nests that we found appear to suffer so heavily, while others, of which we did not know, prospered? I do not think it is a sufficient answer to say that the nests we found were the nests that vermin also would find most easily. It is more probable that when a human being finds and examines a nest he leaves some track or trace that betrays the treasure. A bent twig or a displaced leaf may catch the keen eye of a hungry jackdaw looking down from above. The thought thus suggested discouraged me from nest-finding at the cottage, and in the later years there I was content to be assured by ear that the birds were there: to know all had gone well by seeing young birds being fed, and thus have no knowledge of catastrophes and no share in them.

Many years ago, when I fondly thought that a fence of moderate height with barbed wire on the top would keep out foxes, my waterfowl were raided by a fox. There were about a dozen birds sitting at the time: many of their nests escaped destruction, for the birds appeared in due course with young ones; but the only nests that we had known of and visited, about five in number, were, every one of them, found and robbed by the fox.

Some nests are so exposed that it is surprising that they ever escape. The mistle-thrush builds early, when there is little cover and deciduous trees are still bare. The nest is large and is often placed more aloft than those of the song-thrush: it is therefore very conspicuous. Indeed, it has been said that 'you do not find a mistle-thrush's nest; it finds you.' The mistle-thrush, however, is a bird of some size and high courage: combat is often to be seen between a pair of mistle-thrushes and a jackdaw; and it is probable that sometimes the mistle-thrushes are able to protect the eggs or young.

On returning to a country home after a short absence in spring or early summer, it is natural to visit the nests in which one was interested and to see how they have fared. In the process of growing feathers a light scurf is deposited in the bottom of the nest. If all has gone well with the young birds and they have arrived safely at full feather, the amount of this scurf left in the nest is considerable. In a very open-work nest, such as that of the blackcap, much may have fallen through the bottom of the nest, and the signs may be doubtful; but in most nests they are clear enough, and in a mud-lined nest, such as that of a song-thrush, from which the young have safely fledged, all the scurf is retained. By this sign it is possible to assure ourselves of the success of a nest, which we have found and been unable to revisit till the young have left it.

If birds were to be classified according to methods of incubation, there would be four classes among British birds:

1. The species in which the female does the whole of the sitting on the eggs. In cases where the male is very much brighter in colour than the female, he does not, so far as I have observed, sit upon the eggs. I have never seen a cock chaffinch do so; but is this because the bright plumage might betray the nest, or is it because it is not the custom of the finch tribe for the cock bird to sit? Does the male corn-bunting, whose plumage is as sober as that of the female, take a share in incubation? The blackbird seems to leave the whole process of incubation to the more sober-coloured female; does the male thrush also avoid sitting on the eggs, though he has not the excuse of brighter plumage? When the male and female are alike in plumage, this question can be answered only by seeing one bird take the place of another on the nest. Mr Edmund Selous, I think, has somewhere given an account of seeing nightjars take turns on the eggs; and, if I remember correctly, he has observed that the male bird was perceptibly the more clumsy.

2. Birds of which the males take a share in sitting on the eggs. This is easily observed, as already noted, in the habits of the blackcap; but in most of the warblers the plumage of male and female is alike. Judging by the example of the blackcap, it may be that it is the rule among the warblers for the male to take his share of sitting on the eggs; but I must leave it to those who have had more leisure and opportunity than I to give better information.

3. Birds of which the male does the whole of the sitting on the eggs. The only British bird of this class that occurs to me is the red-necked Phalarope. I have never had the opportunity of seeing a Phalarope alive, and am therefore dependent on books, or on what I have been told. I understand that the female Phalarope is larger and more bright in plumage than the male, and that she insists on her mate enduring the tedium of sitting on the eggs. He has to get his own food, and it seems that he is allowed to leave the nest occasionally for this purpose; but if he dallies or delays he is hunted back on to the nest by the more brilliant and powerful female. It is said that the poor little male deserts very readily, if disturbed, being apparently glad of an excuse to abandon the irksome and undivided duty. It is difficult to imagine how and why this peculiarity developed in the Phalarope. We may suppose a reason for the greater size and power of the female in birds of prey that are carnivorous, such

as the peregrine and sparrow-hawk. The parental instinct of the male may be weak and liable to be overpowered by hunger and natural ferocity: he might occasionally turn upon his own offspring, and the greater size of the female would be a protection against such mishap: but with the gentle Phalarope this cannot be the reason.[1]

4. Birds of which neither the female nor the male sit upon the eggs. The British example of this is the cuckoo; but such observations as I have been able to make of this very odd bird shall be described separately in another chapter. Birds' ways with their nests and eggs illustrate nature's infinite variety. The female lays the eggs. This is, really, the only general statement that can be made on this subject without reserve or qualification.

The following description, which was written by my wife, and has been printed elsewhere, of seeing a goldfinch on its nest, shall end the chapter:

One of the prettiest nests ever found was a goldfinch's. It was in a yew-tree, and the outside of the nest was made of

---

1 There is a story, which has I think appeared in print, of a guest who on several successive visits to country houses had been bored by much talk about birds. Another visit was in prospect where it was thought possible that the subject might be avoided. The chance of this was discussed hopefully with a friend on the day of departure for the visit. The next day, however, the friend received a telegram. It contained three words: 'Red-necked Phalarope.'

green lichen: the lichen you find on beech boles and wooden palings. The inside was incredibly soft to the touch, which was possible only by a very long stretch, so the bamboo ladder was fetched to get a clear sight of it. Then it was found to be lined completely with dandelion 'clock,' each little sphere detached from the many that make the full round of the puff. Another nest, this time lovely in its environment, was again that of a goldfinch. Holding my face deeply into a pyramidal apple-tree in full blossom in order to enjoy the light filtering through the mass of petals that clustered on the boughs so thickly as to shut everything else out, I became aware of the ruby mask of a goldfinch, sitting on her nest not ten inches away. She never stirred; happily I had insinuated myself very gently into this 'world of light.' Neither did I withdraw hastily. I stayed long enough to see how the rose and gold of sunlit apple-blossom could be deepened by this touch of red.

Chapter X

Joy Flights and Joy Sounds

Of all bird songs or sounds known to me there is none that I would prefer to the spring notes of the curlew. I have seen the bird finish its notes on the ground after alighting, but I have not observed if it ever gives them without any flight. As a rule the wonderful notes are uttered on the wing, and are the accompaniment of a graceful flight that has motions of evident pleasure. The notes do not sound passionate: they suggest peace, rest, healing, joy, an assurance of happiness past, present and to come. To listen to curlews on a bright, clear April day, with the fullness of spring still in anticipation, is one of the best experiences that a lover of birds can have. On a still day one can almost feel the air vibrating with the blessed sound. There is no rarity about it where curlews breed: it is to be heard through long days in April, May and far into June. In autumn and winter curlews resort to estuaries and the seashore, and the call note is melancholy; but even at this season on a mild day one may be surprised to hear a single bird give a few of the joy notes, just enough to revive memory of the past spring and to stir anticipation of the next one.

A yet more common and widely distributed pleasure is the spring flight and note of the peewit. It is a real joy flight accompanied by cries of joy: the seeing and hearing of it for the first time in the early months of the year are something longed for and welcomed, as is the first song of a blackbird. Someone in the wholesale trade in birds for food, explaining that peewits were of no use after an early date in the year, said, 'The birds are of no use after they have begun to *lap*.' I suppose, therefore, that the name lapwing is suggested by the joy flight in spring. At other times the peewit gives an impression of plaintiveness.

The peewit or lapwing is a beautiful bird, much praised by farmers for consuming pests on their fields, but it has the misfortune to lay eggs that are an unrivalled delicacy, and these are taken in vast numbers for the English market, not only in this country, but in breeding grounds abroad. For many years I have not seen at Fallodon the vast flocks of peewits that used to visit us in autumn and winter, and which were probably composed largely of foreign birds.

The golden plover, when served on a dish, is so like the peewit in body that it can be distinguished only by the absence of a hind claw. When alive it is very different in appearance and flight. It 'yodels' very pleasantly in the spring. The call note heard frequently in autumn and winter is a single very plaintive whistle.

Redshanks in the breeding season have notes that may also be compared to yodelling; they utter these in a very conspicuous joy flight. Every bird seems to have something that is song, or corresponds to song, in the nesting season. Such is the 'screeling' of swifts as they fly about a village in the late evening; the conversational warbling of swallows as they sit on some perch or convenient place in the sun; wagtails have their little songs, and something of the sort is to be observed with all our common birds. One sound that was common in my boyhood has sadly diminished. The voice of the corncrake is now seldom heard in many places where it used to be common. No one can assert with truth that the sound is melodious; it is in fact very harsh; but it used to enliven many an early summer night in the field adjoining the garden at Fallodon, and I regret that it is heard there no more. Occasionally there is still a corncrake to be heard farther off, but both here and about the Hampshire cottage the bird has in my recollection become rare as a breeding species.

Two other common, but very peculiar, joy sounds shall be mentioned in detail. One is the 'churring' of the nightjar: a most soothing sound, continued for long periods without a break. No one unacquainted with it and hearing it for the first time would guess that the noise was made by a bird at all. It is of that class of stationary, soothing, continuous sounds, such as the hum of a threshing machine, or the noise of waves on the shore heard at a distance, which dispose us to sit still and listen indefinitely.

I have not seen much of nightjars, but I had one curious experience, though not of a joy flight or sound. It was evening, early in September; I had been sitting for some time at the foot of an ash tree that stood solitary in the middle of broad water-meadows. I noticed a bird fly from the branches above me, take something on or near the grass, and return to the tree. This action it repeated several times, and it took little flights about the tree. It was a nightjar, and I enjoyed the opportunity of watching it; for the bird was flying all about me and yet was unconscious of my presence. The bird was silent till at length in one of its flights it passed quite close to and saw me. So near was it that I could see it see me. It gave a piercing shriek, such as I had never heard before from any bird, and flew straight away out of the meadow. For a moment when it discovered me its head had turned in my direction, and the shriek seemed to be uttered *at* me. It suggested not so much fear as rage and loathing: as if the bird was suddenly aware that, unknown to it, a human eye had been watching it, when it believed there was security and privacy. The wife of Candaules,[1] when she knew that the eye of a man not her husband had covertly seen her disrobing, can hardly have felt more horror and indignation than was expressed by that nightjar's shriek.

The other joy sound is the so-called 'drumming' of the snipe. It is said to be made by the outside tail feathers. I have not verified this statement, but I do not doubt it. The sound is made during a prolonged joy flight. The bird flies round and round over a wide area at some height, and every now and then descends in the air at an angle and with accelerated speed; it is in the descent that the sound is made: indeed, this seems to be the whole object of the descending motion, for the bird then immediately recovers itself in the air and resumes its flight. The whole proceeding is one to be watched. The flight has a very happy appearance, but the 'drumming' seems to be performed by the bird in order to find vent for an

[1] Herodotus, i. 8, etc.

exuberance of spirits that cannot be expressed by flight alone. The sound is that of a bleat rather than of a drum, and in some places the snipe is called 'air-goat' in consequence. The snipe has another note that I have heard only at the same season as the 'drumming.' This is a very monotonous 'chucking' noise. It may be uttered on the wing, but the bird takes pleasure in doing it on the ground. When I was lunching out on the Broads one day in late spring, a snipe stood in view on a heap of cut reeds and made this 'chucking' noise till it became wearisome. This snipe did nothing else, but I have heard the noise made on the ground in a water-meadow, and have presently seen a snipe, presumably the same bird, rise up from the spot and do its joy flight and drum. Whether the female snipe makes this tiresome note as well as the male, I do not know. It has no resemblance to the ordinary note uttered at all seasons when the bird rises from the ground.

A real drumming is that of a woodpecker. There was a poplar with a dead top in front of the Hampshire cottage, and to one dead bit of the tree a lesser spotted woodpecker would come more than once a day in the spring and drum. From the doorway of the sitting room the bird could be seen clinging to a dead upright branch of the tree, and the noise was loud, but it was not possible to distinguish the motions of the head. The sound is, I suppose, made by repeated hard and very rapid strokes of the bill on resonant dead wood, but one cannot distinguish separate taps. It is like a sound made in one continuous piece, and reminds me in miniature of the 'roar' of a stag.

This is the only woodpecker that I have observed intimately, though the laughter of the green wood-pecker, from which it gets the name of 'yaffle,' is familiar, and it is the commonest of all our wood-peckers; but I have never heard it drum. Its flight gives the impression of weakness, rising and falling, so that one cannot imagine it to be capable of any sustained flying. Common though it is in the southern parts of England, there is something in the colouring of the green woodpecker, something foreign, that every time one sees it gives the impression of looking at an uncommon bird.

The larger spotted woodpecker I have seen only casually, but I found one that, contrary to the habit of its kind, was not at all shy. It was among some wild birch trees on an open moor in Sutherland. It was searching some soft rotten tops of the birches, and took no notice of me at ten yards' distance, though we were in full view of each other. I had a good look at it through field glasses. The month was April, but I saw no sign of any mate. It was interesting to see a bird of this species so far north in so wild a place, and to find it so tame.

As we get old and go less afield – and particularly

if sight fails, so that we have to say literally and physically,

The things that I have seen I now can see no more,

– we like to recall with the inward eye some aspects of the flight of birds. One is that of gulls on a fine day wheeling slowly and peacefully high in the air. This seems to be done for sheer enjoyment. W. H. Hudson, remembering the number of large birds that wheeled above him in the Argentine when he was a boy, regretted that in England the upper air was so empty. Gulls, by this sustained and lofty pleasure, do at some times and in some places redeem our upper air from this charge of emptiness. Gulls in stormy weather steering a course across a bay or along the coast may be seen to take advantage of the shelter of waves; they will fly along the lee side of a wave, then, to keep their course, cross over its crest, and immediately continue in the lee of the next wave; thus using the waves to shelter and ease their flight. The spectacle of gulls following and keeping up with a steamer without any beat of wings is well known, but is, I am told, simple of explanation.

The evening flight of starlings over their chosen roosting place in autumn and winter is one of the marvels of flying. The birds assemble, small parties coming to the chosen spot from any direction after the business of the day is over. They then fly at speed above the roosting place: a vast globe, it may be, of some thousands of birds. They fly close together, and there are many evolutions and swift turns, yet there is no collision: the impulse to each quick movement or change of direction seems to seize every bird simultaneously. It is as if for the time being each bird had ceased to be a separate entity and had become a part of one sentient whole: one great body, the movement of whose parts was co-ordinated by one impulse or one will affecting them all at the same moment. For some time this wonderful performance continues, then as the globe passes over the laurels a little avalanche of starlings descends, making a rushing noise as it penetrates the stiff leaves. Party after party of starlings now detaches itself and descends each time that the globe passes over the spot, till at length there is but one small party left flying, and this, too, presently descends. There are now hundreds, or it may be thousands, of birds in the evergreens, and for a while there is fuss and chatter; so loud is the noise that I have known it mistaken at a little distance for the sound of a waterfall. I have spoken of laurels, because it is these that the starlings choose at Fallodon, but they may select any thicket of evergreens. It is only occasionally that starlings choose a winter gathering and roosting place at Fallodon. If the spot selected is not near the house the birds are not disturbed, for it is very interesting to watch this evening performance. But once they chose the laurels past which ran the approach to the house. In such a position the stench of the fouled shrubs and ground became an intolerable nuisance: the laurels were cut down, which is not only the most merciful, but the most effective way of persuading the starlings to go elsewhere. It is not apparent that this evening flight of starlings serves any purpose except that of pleasure, but it occurs in late autumn and winter, and cannot therefore be quite analogous to the joy flights of spring and the pairing season.

A very extraordinary noise is made by the black-throated diver. It suggests to me the crying of a child in agony:[1] it is often made at a great height in the air. As this peculiar and painful noise ceases after the breeding season, it is, I suppose, a joy sound on the part of the bird. Whether the flight is a joy flight I have not been able to observe. I have only seen and heard black-throated divers at the very end of the breeding season, on the rare occasions when I have been fortunate enough to get to western parts of the Highlands for sea-trout fishing in July. The red-throated diver has similar habits, but the cry, though very frequent at the same season, is not so strange.

It is remarkable that both these birds should fly so

1 The same comparison is made in books.

much and so high. They do not use flight as a means of escape: for this, if pursued, they rely upon diving, as if flight were too laborious; but for pleasure or going at will from place to place, they are great and lofty fliers.

With the great northern diver I have, to my regret, no acquaintance at all.

Cormorants have a peculiar habit with their wings: they will stand on a rock for a long time with the wings outspread and motionless, as if they represented something in heraldry.

A keeper of the waterfowl in St James's Park told me many years ago of an amusing misapprehension which this habit of the cormorant had caused. A spectator, who had noticed a cormorant standing with outstretched wings, rang the bell of the keeper's cottage in order to summon him and to tell him that some one had 'wired' one of his birds.

This action and attitude of cormorants gives the impression that they are drying their wings, but I do not know why a cormorant's wings should get more wet or need more drying than those of other diving birds. Cormorants are at times unwilling or unable to fly. A retriever of mine swam after one of these birds on a small open and isolated pool in the Orkneys; but the bird refused to fly. There was no reason to suppose that it was injured and when I passed the spot later in the day it had gone. A cormorant was sitting on a wooden fence that came down to the edge of a salmon pool. It remained as I fished the pool down towards it: not till I was within casting distance did it move, and then only down from the fence into the pool, hitting my line as it descended. It is possible that cormorants cannot fly when gorged with food, and have to wait till digestion has restored their balance.

There is a tendency for bright colour to be inconspicuous in flight. We are not conscious of the gorgeous plumage of a cock pheasant, or even of the incredible splendour of a mandarin drake, when the birds are on the wing. The colours of the kingfisher are an exception to this; the bird flashes like a jewel as it flies. When the sharp note that it utters is heard when it is on the wing, our eyes search for a glimpse of something brilliant. It has to be admitted, however, that this is due partly to the angle of vision. A kingfisher is generally seen from above or on a level with us, as it flies low between the banks of a stream or swiftly over a water-meadow. Yet I think in the matter of brilliance when flying, the kingfisher is something of an exception to a general rule.

To return now, in conclusion, to the proper subject of this chapter – joy flights. The main purpose served by flight is utilitarian, to enable birds to reach feeding places, to escape from enemies, to change their climate; but they also use flight to express blissful well-being; by this as well as by song they are gifted beyond all other creatures to convey to the mind of man the existence in nature of happiness and joy. How far this is consciously felt by birds I will not discuss: it is good for man to watch it, to listen to it, and to know that it is here.

There is yet another exhibition of bird happiness which is neither flight nor sound: it may be called a joy attitude. A good example of it is to be seen when a blackbird suns itself on a lawn. The bird may be observed lying on its side with one wing uplifted, so that the warm sunshine may penetrate through the small soft feathers of the body. The appearance is that of a bird ill or wounded or in some distress, but it is in fact enjoying a sun bath. One of the most pleasing and attractive sights that I ever beheld was on a day in June: the air was unusually cold for the time of year and the breeze was chill, but the sun shone full into the chalk-pit close to the Hampshire cottage. I was lingering there to enjoy the warmth of this sheltered sunny place. A family of long-tailed tits flew into the chalk-pit and settled on a young ash tree that rose above the surrounding blackthorns. The little birds were at once conscious of the warmth and disposed themselves in various sun attitudes on the branches of the tree. There they remained, their usually ceaseless activity suspended for a while in motionless enjoyment.

Chapter XI

The Cuckoo and the Sparrow

These two birds are each the object of some degree of popular disapproval. The habits of one of them are very uncommon; those of the other are particularly common; but the ways of both to human notions are displeasing.

The cuckoo makes no nest: it dumps its egg, the hatching of it and the care of its young on some pair of birds of another species, whose domestic affairs are thereby spoilt. The cuckoo has no family life, and is said to be polyandrous. All this has aroused the disapproval of mankind. I do not know how it has been proved that our cuckoos are polyandrous: the males certainly seem to be much more numerous than the females; but it has to be remembered that the familiar notes of the male correspond to the song of male birds; these notes would therefore be heard much more in the breeding season than the notes of the female even if the two sexes were equal in number. The female cuckoo has notes in the breeding season that are as distinctive as those of the male among the notes of other birds; but these female notes are much more seldom heard. In fact, to many even of the people who live in the country, these notes are not a familiar sound, and, when heard, are not known to be those of a cuckoo. They are sometimes called the 'water-bubbling' notes; and I cannot improve on this description. They seem to me to be used solely as a mating call. I once had a particularly good example of the female cuckoo's call. I was sitting under a lime tree at the Hampshire cottage; the spreading branches concealed me from outside view, but looking out from beneath them much could be seen. A cuckoo came flying and lit on the branch of a poplar only a few yards in front. Having chosen its perch, the bird uttered the loud 'water-bubbling' notes. A male cuckoo was immediately heard at some distance; it came, cuckooing vehemently as it flew, and lit on the branch by the side of the first bird. There what Chaucer calls a 'spring observance' took place. In this instance there was no sign of a second male in the neighbourhood;

there was nothing, therefore, to suggest that the two cuckoos were not paired like monogamous birds. Sometimes, however, the 'water-bubbling' note provokes the cuckooing and pursuit of more than one male bird. The familiar 'cuckoo' is thus, on some occasions, an answer to the call of the female; but generally, like other bird song, it is an expression of sheer joy, vigour, challenge or excitement.

The habits of the cuckoo are so well known that nothing shall be said about them here, except to recall two or three observations that may have some points of special interest.

Once in late May or early June, while driving along a country lane, a cuckoo flew out of the hedge with much perturbation. We stopped to examine the spot, and found there a nest not quite finished, but sufficiently advanced to be identified as that of a dunnock. I was not to be in the neighbourhood again for some time: I asked my companion, who was resident, to ascertain what happened to the nest. He informed me afterwards that it had been completed and a cuckoo's egg had been laid with those of the dunnock. This suggests that cuckoos mark down nests in advance.

The experience of a pair of pied wagtails that nested every year on the Hampshire cottage is an example of the persecution inflicted by a cuckoo. For some years the wagtails were unmolested; then came a year when a cuckoo discovered them. Their nest was in a tangled mass of creeper that filled a small alcove on the front of the cottage. The cuckoo placed an egg in the nest and the wagtails hatched the egg and reared a young cuckoo, to the exclusion of their own offspring. When this task was completed, the wagtails built a second nest in ivy on the back of the cottage. Again the cuckoo put an egg in the nest, and the unfortunate wagtails reared a second monster. The next year the wagtails made a nest once more in the same creeper-filled alcove. After three or four eggs had been laid I found a cuckoo at the nest: no egg had then been laid by the cuckoo, but the wagtails deserted and never built on the cottage again.

Cuckoos' eggs found in nests on or close to the cottage were all of the same type, resembling the eggs of pied wagtails; but they were found in various nests; robins and sedge-warblers and dunnocks were used as foster parents, as well as pied wagtails. There was one exceptional experience with a sedge-warbler. I disturbed the bird on its nest, and a casual glance showed that there was only one egg: I withdrew immediately, fearing that I had disturbed the bird in the act of laying and that it might desert. On returning at the next weekend, I found to my satisfaction that the sedge-warbler was sitting. I put the bird off, expecting to see a full clutch of sedge-warbler eggs; but there was still only one egg, and a more careful look showed it to be that of a cuckoo. Now the sedge-warbler would not have been sitting unless it had laid a full clutch of its own eggs; all these had disappeared, and the presumption is that the cuckoo had removed them. Every cuckoo's egg laid close to the cottage in any year, and possibly in several successive years, would be those of one and the same bird. Yet this is the only instance in which I found a cuckoo's egg alone in a nest: and why she should have departed, on this occasion, from her usual practice of removing no egg, or only one from a nest, is not apparent. The sedge-warbler, it may be added, hatched the egg and reared the cuckoo.

The precocious prowess of the infant cuckoo in ejecting its companions and the method by which it does this are now matter of common knowledge, admitted and established as facts, and even photographed. Jenner described the process accurately towards the end of the eighteenth century, and from that time it was open to anyone who doubted Jenner's account to test it by observation or experiment. Yet more than a hundred years after Jenner's statement was made I read a signed letter in the Press denying that an infant cuckoo ever did, or could act so. This denial is a good example of that failing in human nature that leads people to prefer to deny rather than to know. This disposition is often met with, but its opposite, the inclination to believe, or to assert without proof, is still more common. Both these tendencies are obstructions to scientific progress and to the spread of truth.

The voice of the cuckoo, apart from its habits, has always been popular. The old English verse, 'Summer is icumen in,' is a warm welcome to the bird. The instance quoted in a previous chapter, where Wordsworth transfers the melancholy of his own mood to the cry of the cuckoo, is an exception. Elsewhere the cuckoo's note is a cause of rejoicing, a suggestion of happiness.

Every year it is welcome because it is so intimately associated with the most beautiful season of the year. It is a strange cry that does not blend with other sounds of nature, but interrupts them or breaks a silence, like a human voice:

> Breaking the silence of the seas
> Among the furthest Hebrides.

I have never been in the Hebrides in cuckoo-time, but I have found cuckoos particularly abundant in June in the glens of the Western Highlands of Scotland. As the season advances the bird plays various tricks with its voice; the straightforward, clear 'two-fold shout' may be broken up into imperfect syllables. The cuckoo also makes an odd noise, a gruff chuckling sound, that has been described as goblin laughter.

It is said that the old cuckoos leave the country in

late summer before the young are ready to migrate. The young birds therefore find their own way without any guidance from their species. There does not seem to be anything remarkable in this: a great stream of migration making south, and birds of all sorts are drawn along it. Migration is an instinct, inherited, and impelling birds to do what countless generations of their kind have done. Sense of direction is instinctive too: it does not seem to me more wonderful that a young cuckoo should, without guidance, make the annual journey of its kind, than that a chaffinch should without instruction build in its first season a perfect nest.

Now let sparrows be considered. Except in towns we would rather be without them. Sparrows will chirp in the early morning in such a manner as to be a nuisance, while other birds are singing. Their very chirp is harsh amongst other chirps: to song, it is an offence. Their nests are so untidy as to be eyesores. Incapable of making anything but a loose and formless nest themselves, they often appropriate the compact structure of a house-martin, and in converting this to their own use deface it with untidy straw. They multiply exceedingly and damage crops of grain: they despoil crocus flowers. Their familiarity is offensive because it is combined with a distrust that is almost ostentatious. At the Hampshire cottage food used to be put on the lawn in front of the little sitting room.

Numbers of birds came to it; the party used to include blackbirds, thrushes, chaffinches, bullfinches, pied wagtails, robins, dunnocks, great, blue, and marsh tits, and sometimes a pair of nuthatches. Some of these birds that were regular guests became fairly tame; all of them gained by degrees a little confidence. Several pairs of sparrows were always about; never would one of these feed while anyone was looking on; but as soon as I was behind a tree or had gone to a little distance, they would descend upon the food. Compared to the other birds, they had the manners of thieves, and snatched surreptitiously. The sparrow is a very unattractive bird compared to others that are akin to it. What is there to be said in favour of it? This, to begin with: it is a bird; and, being a bird, it has feathers, and having feathers it has not been able to avoid a certain degree of beauty. The cock sparrow, if carefully considered, is a beautiful bird. Sparrows are also very affectionate to mates and nestlings. The cock sparrow takes a strenuous and devoted part in rearing the young. Then it must be admitted that sparrows are very clever birds; in one respect there is something uncanny about their cleverness. The hand of man is against them, and yet they take no trouble to conceal their nests. On the contrary, by excessive untidiness with feathers and straw, they thrust their nests upon man's attention; yet, in spite of this, sparrows thrive. How is it done? Chiefly, I think, by choosing situations for the nest that make man disinclined to go to it. A sparrow's nest can be discovered without search, but cannot be reached generally without trouble.

There has lately been an instance at Fallodon of the cleverness of sparrows. It has been the custom for several years to keep a basket of bread in the greenhouse, that it may be at hand to feed the waterfowl. More than one pair of chaffinches nest near the greenhouse, but they have never discovered the bread. Three years ago a pair of sparrows nested in the garden. There had been none there for some time after horses were no longer kept. It did not take these sparrows long, though their nest was fifty yards away, to discover the bread, and how to get in and out of the greenhouse through the top ventilator. The moment anyone entered they flew out at the top, without losing their way. The neighbouring chaffinches have not made the discovery, not even since the sparrows came and showed the way. Yet chaffinches are as fond as sparrows of feeding their young with soft bread.

A man of business was once being sounded as to the capacity of other prominent persons in his own or in allied industries in the North of England. 'What about X?' he was asked. 'X doesn't *miss* much,' was the reply. So it can be said of the sparrow, that it doesn't miss much. This faculty, combined with domestic virtue and a robust body, enables the sparrow to hold so very much more than its own in spite of man's antagonism.

Chapter XII

On Taming Birds

This is an age of curiosity. There is a desire to know about the private life of people who are much before the public; and birds, as well as men and women, are the subject of more curious and particular observation than they have ever endured before.

Papers like those of Mr Burkitt in *British Birds* and *The Irish Naturalist* show how much there is to discover about the private life even of the commonest birds, such as the robin and the wren. The time and patience required to make these observations are immense, but the result is to add to our knowledge of birds that are in our gardens every day of the year, and to quicken our interest in them.

My own experience has been mainly with robins.

Several of these were tamed at different times, not with any intention of scientific observation, but solely for the pleasure of being on terms of intimacy with birds in a free and natural state. None of these robins were quite close to the house: none of them became house birds, nor were they induced to lead an artificial life. They were visited once every day, each in its own territory, and offered meal-worms; but except for this supplement to their natural food, there was nothing to disturb or distort their natural habits.

The first robin had a small white feather on the right wing by which it was easy to identify him. This freak feather was constant; either it was never moulted or it reappeared after each moult. His territory included both sides of one end of a pond. The water was about ten yards wide, and on either side were trees and bushes. The bird had a good strip of territory on each side of the pond, but more on the west than on the east side. In the winter of 1921–22 he would sit on my fingers and eat meal-worms out of a little box held open on the hand. In the nesting season he was feeding young birds: about the middle of July he disappeared and was not seen again till well on in August, when he presented himself once more and came on the hand as usual, and reoccupied precisely the same territory. Here he remained tame, but alone, till the spring of 1923, when a female was admitted to the territory. She would make a small note and he would feed her with meal-worms, just as if she were a young bird. If I appeared and held out the box when he was not near, the female would sit in a bush uttering the little notes till he came and fed her. She never offered to help herself. About the middle of July he disappeared, but again showed himself in the latter part of August. The following months were a repetition of those of other years, including the admission and feeding of a female in the spring of 1924. In 1924 there was the same disappearance for the moult in July after the breeding season. In August he reappeared, with the white feather either still intact or renewed after moulting. It had become convenient to distinguish this bird by the name of 'White Feather', and so he was always called. After he reappeared this time there was trouble about territory, and eventually the east side of the pond was annexed by another robin, and White Feather was restricted entirely to the west side. Here he was visited and fed. He had now become very tame, and after satisfying his appetite would sometimes sit on the hand so long that it was necessary to give him a gentle hint to go. On the last day of the year 1924, he came to me at the usual spot; after that I never saw him again, and his place was taken by another robin. I searched in the hope that White Feather might only have been driven farther west; but there was no sign, and I fear that there had been combat to the death.

The observation of another robin showed similar habits with certain variations.

There is a white seat by another pond, where it is the habit for someone to sit about midday to feed such waterfowl as care to come out of the water for bread. On the right of this seat and close to it is a clump of dogwood. Here in February 1924 a robin and his mate were tamed. The male bird would sit on the hand and eat several meal-worms; the female would only perch for a moment, snatch a single meal-worm at a time and fly off with it. As spring advanced the female ceased to feed herself, but sat in the dogwood, uttering the plaintive note, and was fed attentively by the male. In time the female ceased coming to the seat, and the male would pack his beak with meal-worms, fly with them over the water to some bushes a hundred yards away, and return time after time to get more. The nest was evidently in the distant bushes, but I made no search for it, lest by finding I should betray it to some enemy. In July the male also disappeared, and it was not till September that I found him expecting to be fed, not at the seat, but in the bushes near the site of the nest. He was as tame as before, and for several days endeavoured to come to me at the seat. But the dogwood was in possession of another robin, that attacked him furiously. Finally he gave up the attempt to come to me at the seat, and it was a recognised thing that he was fed in the bushes at a safe distance from the virago in the dogwood. So matters continued through the autumn and winter. The bird in the dogwood never came on my hand, and whether it was the female of the previous spring, or indeed whether it was a female at all, I cannot be certain. In the spring of 1925, however, the tame robin was admitted to the seat and to the dogwood, where it fed a mate. It seems probable that this mate was the same bird that drove him from the seat in the autumn and had been in the dogwood territory throughout the winter; but as it was not hand-tame and had no distinct mark, I cannot be sure of this. In the nesting season the female went out of sight as before. The last time I saw the male, in July that year, he was pursued by two speckled and importunate young birds: he gave them a meal-worm or two from my box, but seemed more anxious to escape from them than to feed them. After the moult he reappeared in the bushes as in 1924, and there was an exact repetition of the proceedings of the previous year: exclusion from the seat and dogwood territory till the early part of 1926, then admission to it, and feeding of a female in the dogwood. In April there was trouble: the tame robin appeared with his breast feathers dreadfully disordered: he held his ground so for some days in April, and I fed him daily: then one day no robin came to the seat and the proffered box of meal-worms. High up in a young tree close by a robin was singing very loud and bold: I stood underneath with the box of meal-worms open on outstretched hand. All my overtures were ignored; the robin was a stranger, and sang there daily thereafter with an indifference that seemed ostentatious. My white-seat robin was never seen again. The new bird never was tame, and remained an example of:

> The simple rule, the good old plan,
> That those should take who have the power,
> And those should keep who can.

Whether the conqueror possessed himself of the mate as well as the territory of the tame bird I could not tell.

Besides the white-seat robin I had three others that were hand-tame in the winter of 1925–26. Their territories adjoined and apparently met in a large spiræa bush. Two and sometimes all three birds came to this bush together, and whenever this was so, feeding was impossible; each bird as it perched on my hand was knocked off by another before it could eat. The incessant combats were wearisome, almost disgusting, and I had to manoeuvre to get each bird fed peacefully in its own territory. One of these birds I judged to be a female, for it would snatch meal-worms from the box and not sit on my hand and eat quietly as the other two birds did. By March one of the males was settled in a territory that adjoined the east of a greenhouse. He was a particularly delightful bird and very tame. His singing place was high up in a sycamore tree. I would hold out the box; the singing would stop; there would be a short pause of silence, and then he would fly straight down to my hand and sit there, till satisfied; when he would again fly up to his sycamore perch and sing. If he saw me in the greenhouse he would come to me through the open ventilator at the top. Once after eating a few meal-worms he sang while on my hand: a full and proper song, loud and sustained, very ear-piercing at such close quarters. 'White Feather' often sang a few notes before he left the hand, but this bird is the only one that has ever treated my hand as a real singing perch. I could not discover that he had a mate, and in April he disappeared, though I saw no sign of his territory being disputed and no other robin sang in his place.

Of the other two robins, the one that 'snatched' was, as I had supposed, a female; they paired; their two territories, which were next to each other, were amalgamated:[1] as in old days a king would marry the queen or heiress to the throne of a neighbouring country and combine the two kingdoms in one realm.

I was now beginning to write this book and made

---

1 It may be noticed that in the case of the white-seat robin, two adjoining territories, that had been disputed, were amalgamated each nesting season.

some notes at the time with a view to giving an account of these two birds. At the end of January 1926 there was an amelioration in their respective attitudes – amity would be too strong a word, but they began to tolerate each other. Their territory came up to the western end of the greenhouse. In front of the entrance is a four-cornered pedestal of clipped yew: at first neither bird could come on the flat top of this pedestal without a fight if the other was there. Towards the end of January, however, each bird would allow the other to come on to the yew at the same time. I fed them there by hand, but any attempt by one bird to feed at the same moment as the other was resented; they took turns. At this time the attitude of each to the other seemed to be one of reluctant toleration: as if they felt some compelling force of nature was obliging them to forego the dislike and animosity that each still felt towards the other.

In March the male began to feed the female. Even now their manners were not affectionate. The male fed his mate assiduously, but briskly, as if it were a piece of business that *had* to be done. There was no love making; no courting or display by the male; none of those insinuating advances or pretty provocations on the part of the female that are usual in other species; only the little notes that were understood by the male and treated by him as a demand for food.

The nest was about eight feet up in thick ivy on

the kitchen garden wall, about fifty yards from the yew. On the 23rd April the young birds were very audible; both parents were very busy feeding them and would come on to my hand together and take meal-worms; but the female still snatched from the box and did not stand quietly on my hand like the male.

On the 11th May both birds were feeding fledged and clamorous young.

On the 15th May the male bird was again feeding the female; a young bird appeared at the foot of the yew, apparently desirous of being fed, but it was ignored. On the 16th May only the male was seen; he showed no great eagerness for food, but twice came on to my hand and flew away with two meal-worms each time, presumably to feed the unseen female. On the 23rd May both birds came to me in the greenhouse (they had acquired the habit some weeks ago of following me in through the door); the female was there fed by the male, but also came once on to my hand and took one meal-worm herself. On the 24th May I could find only the male; he was singing on a cypress near the yew, and was at first indifferent to my offer of food; eventually he came down to my hand, ate one meal-worm and took two more in his beak at once and flew off with them, a sure sign that he was feeding something, presumably the female still. After the 24th May neither bird was seen again. When the moulting season had passed a robin appeared and sang in the territory, but as it showed nothing but fear or annoyance when I offered it meal-worms, it was evidently a strange bird. The end of 'White Feather' and of the white-seat robin, I fear, was each a tragedy; but what happened to this last pair of robins was for six months blank mystery.[1]

Any male robin can be tamed; such at least is my experience. The bird is first attracted by crumbs of bread thrown on the ground; then a meal-worm is thrown to it; then a box – such as one of the small metal boxes in which chemists sell lozenges – is placed open on the ground with meal-worms in it. When the bird has become used to this, the next step is to kneel down and place the back of one hand flat upon the ground with the box open on the upturned palm, and the fingers projecting beyond the box. This is the most difficult stage, but robins will risk their lives for meal-worms, and the bird will soon face the fingers and stand on them. The final stage, that of getting the bird to come on to the hand when raised above the ground, is easy. The whole process may be a matter of only two or three days in hard weather, when birds are hungry; and when once it has been accomplished the robin does not lose its tameness: confidence has

---

1 A further account of these robins is given in a note at the end of this chapter.

been established and does not diminish when weather becomes mild and food plentiful.

A robin's method of feeding is to pick up a meal-worm crosswise in its beak and hold it thus for a second or two; then suddenly – there is no meal-worm: the act of swallowing is so quick that it is hardly perceptible. The first meal-worms are taken one after the other with little delay; but after these the bird has long pauses and stands pensively on the hand. In cold weather it is disagreeable to keep the bare hand extended so long, but one does not like to disturb the bird. The last meal-worm is generally taken to a bush or to the ground to be eaten, and this is a sign that the bird is satisfied. I find that four tame robins are as many as are convenient; to visit each and feed it in its own territory once a day is a sufficient demand upon leisure. If natural food is very plentiful a robin may be satisfied with four meal-worms, but the usual number is about nine; the most that I ever knew to be taken by one bird at one standing was twenty-two. Each meal-worm is eaten whole and alive. After several have been swallowed the sensations in the crop may account for the long pauses the bird makes, and its thoughtful aspect.

One note used by robins is a very small, high sound, a note such as we might imagine to be made if a tiny bow were drawn across a single fine hair stretched on a tiny violin. This note expresses annoyance at the approach of another robin to the territory. It is a very inward note and seems to express the emotion of the bird that makes it, rather than to be a warning or a challenge. This note is often made when the bird is on the hunt.

Another note is a short warble, a smaller sound than the full song; it is very sweet in tone, but is in fact a warning or a challenge to a robin in neighbouring territory, and is either in answer to or is answered by the robin to which it is addressed. This warble is frequently given when standing on the hand, and the intention and reason of it are always apparent.

A fight between two robins is a serious affair. One cold January day 'White Feather' came into the territory of another tame robin, when it was on my hand. A furious combat ensued at my feet, and when it was over there were pitiful-looking little dark feathers left strewn upon the snow. So many were they that had I found them without having seen how they came there, I should certainly have thought that some bird had been killed on the spot.

During a cold spell in January 1924, a coal-tit became interested in the feeding of one of the tame robins. It would sit in the bushes very close to me and attentively watch the robin feeding on my hand. After some days I induced the coal-tit to trust me. Its method of dealing with a meal-worm was very different from that of the robins. The tit would perch on my hand, select a meal-worm and fly off to a branch with it. There it placed a foot on the meal-worm and devoured it in pieces. When offered chopped suet in the box, it would sit on my hand and eat it bit by bit, but it invariably took a meal-worm away to be dealt with on a firm hard perch. When we had got on comfortable and confident terms with each other, the habit of the coal-tit was to wait for me on the branches of a big larch tree near the entrance of the greenhouse, from which I used to emerge with the box of meal-worms. Having fed it at the larch one afternoon, I proceeded to some wooded ground about two hundred yards away, where there were overgrown laurels. On these I set to work with a saw. Presently I noticed a coal-tit watching me: I stopped sawing, held out the open box, and the tit came at once on to my hand. It remained near me, while I worked for an hour or more, and it was given a meal-worm occasionally. When I left the laurels it followed me back, flying from bush to bush alongside my path, till we got to the larch, where I gave it a final feed before going up to the house.

I hoped for permanent friendly relations with this coal-tit, and put up several boxes that might attract it or its mate, when it had one, to nest; but before spring came it disappeared and has never returned. The contrast between the ways of the tit and those of the robins was very marked. The tit could follow me anywhere unmolested; no robin could do so without trespassing on another territory and being involved in a fight.

My wife once trained even a wren to come into the house and take food from her fingers. It was interesting to note how different was its method of approach from that of a tame robin. The latter came bold and straight; the wren secretively with zigzag hopping.

With leisure in an uninterrupted country life much more might be done in taming wild birds. Indeed, I have known of one garden, though I never had the good fortune to see it, where the owner by patience and regular habits succeeded in keeping many wild birds of several varieties on terms of intimacy with him, more remarkable than any described here.

More birds are to be seen, free and tame, in London than on any country estate. In London black-headed gulls, that are entirely wild birds, come in numbers in autumn and winter, and will feed, or at any rate snatch food from the hand. Several varieties of interesting waterfowl, especially pochards and tufted ducks, may be seen close to us, and yet free; and the sparrows and wood-pigeons positively invite attention. Now and then one comes across someone who is taking full advantage of the opportunities offered by the tameness of London birds. I met a man in Regent Park one day who was feeding sparrows on his hand.

I stood beside him; a wood-pigeon was walking about, a few yards away. 'Can you get that wood-pigeon to come on to your hand?' 'Oh, yes,' he said, and turning towards the bird held out his hand with a gesture, deliberate but smooth and quiet. The pigeon flew up, and fed with its pink feet planted on his hand. We had some conversation in which he gave me some information about grey and black squirrels, and made some interesting comments of his own upon them. When we parted I left with the inward assurance that here was someone who never lacked interest in his leisure, and who had one satisfaction that no one can have in the country – that of being completely trusted by a free wood-pigeon.

It may be of interest to give some account of experiments in rearing tame partridges. The eggs are hatched under a bantam, which is shut up with the young birds in a coop every night; but in order that the partridges may be brought up to a free life, they and their foster parent range at will during the day. Care and attention are needed to make and keep the birds hand-tame, but if the foster mother is tame there is no great difficulty in getting the little birds to feed from the hand. Provided the garden is free from vermin, all goes well in the early stages. It is when the partridges are more than half grown that trouble begins. Their instinct to roost on the ground in the open asserts itself; so perhaps does the instinct of the bantam to roost aloft in a bush or tree. It becomes daily more difficult to get the birds into any safe enclosure at night. Then for a period the brown owls raid the young covey. Out of a promising covey of sixteen, some years ago, half were lost in this way. They would fly over the garden fence into a small field with many trees, and in the morning there would be one bird less. Feathers showed that the mischief was done at the roosting place. On the flat lead that went round the roof, three skeletons with young partridge feathers attached were found. Each body had been placed on its back and picked clean, and there was no doubt that it was the brown owls that took the birds to the roof. Every covey that I have reared has suffered more or less in the same way at the same stage of its growth. When the birds are full-grown the losses cease, possibly, because they then fly over the trees to roost in more open country, less searched by the owls; I suppose too that full-grown partridges are not usually the prey of brown owls.

The eight survivors of the covey here referred to were the tamest and most attractive of any birds that I ever had. An account of them was written about five years ago to supplement an interesting description of the play of wild partridges that had appeared in a previous letter from someone else. This is an extract from my letter to *The Field*:

One covey of eight birds grew up absolutely without fear or distrust of man, and it was possible to watch all their ways. There is a deodar on the lawn with branches touching the ground, and round the circle of these branches two birds would sometimes run in opposite directions and 'set to partners' when they met in the way described by Mr Gordon Clark. And many other forms of play they had. Indeed, play was a considerable element in their life. In dry weather they dusted in the flower beds, and it was very attractive to watch this, standing close above them, and seeing a partridge sometimes lying on its side indulging itself with sun-warmed dry earth, and looking up with one bright eye with no fear in it. After sunset, when strong on the wing, they spread out on the lawn, standing erect, taking little short runs and calling. Then all together they would take one long flight, over shrubs and trees into large grass fields, where they lit and went to roost, well in the open, away from all hedges, and leaving no trail by which animals of prey could track them from their evening feeding to their resting place. All this evening procedure was, of course, exactly in the well-known manner of wild partridges, and I see no reason to doubt that all their ways of play, etc., were those habitual to wild birds also. Each morning the tame covey would be back in the garden again, but my tame coveys never stayed beyond October. Sooner or later in that month they fell in with wild birds, or became restless; their returns to the garden became irregular; they seemed to have an irresistible impulse to change their ground. Not even hemp seed would keep them at home, and they became merged in the wild stock. One year a covey was satisfied with a migration of about six hundred yards to the keeper's cottage, where they presented themselves for food every day till the pairing season, but with that, and one other exception, the tame coveys were never certainly traced.

If only a tame covey would remain till the pairing season, and if one pair would nest in the garden and rear a new generation of tame birds! But never have I had this good fortune. A covey reared in 1925 did, indeed, continue to visit the garden and feed from the hand throughout the winter. They left once in the end of September, but eventually appeared at the woodman's cottage about three-quarters of a mile distant. Here they were recognised and caught, and ignominiously brought back to the garden in a hamper. This escapade seemed to satisfy their instinct for migration: they flew away every evening, but returned some time in the course of the next day. In February they became very irregular; and finally all deserted me, though one bird that was long in finding a mate came alone to be fed as late as April. None of my tame partridges have ever come back or been met with anywhere in a recognisable state of tameness after the breeding season. Wild companions make them completely wild. With waterfowl, happily, it is otherwise. Tame birds that go away to breed often return, and are still tame; sometimes they bring or attract wild birds of their own kind, but the result is not to make the tame birds wild, but the wild birds tame.

This contrast between tame partridges and tame waterfowl is very evident when wild partridges follow a tame covey into the garden. The wild ones give the tame no peace till they have unsettled them, and sooner or later they induce them not to return after the night's absence. It must be remembered, however, that in the instances I have in mind, the tame covey has consisted entirely of young birds; the wild birds have been adult without a covey of their own. The covey instinct would make them desire to annex the tame birds, and their age and experience would give them the ascendancy.

With the waterfowl there is no covey instinct, and many of the tame birds are old and experienced in wild life. The wild ones have, therefore, neither the same desire nor the same power to influence the tame birds as has been the case with my partridges.

As indicated in the letter quoted above, the evening flight of partridges is evidently a protective habit. They roost in the open, out of the track of hedge-hunting vermin; and they fly to this spot so as to leave no trail for vermin to follow.

Any unusual gesture or movement affronts or frightens tame birds, but otherwise they seem to recognise people by clothes more than by anything else. The robins, it is true, are indifferent to clothes; they will

come to the meal-worm box, whatever the garb of
the person who offers it. But the waterfowl are
perceptibly less tame if I wear dark clothes, though
my whistle and gestures are familiar to them. In the
long days of summertime the sunset feed is not till
after dinner, and it is desirable when visiting them to
conceal evening clothes (if one has dressed for dinner)
with a light-coloured overcoat.

A pair of swallows used to nest in the little wooden
porch at the Hampshire cottage. One Saturday afternoon, when I knew that there were young birds, I
had mounted a few steps of a small ladder to feel if
all was well with the nest. The parent birds, coming
to feed the young, caught me with my hand in the
nest. I withdrew myself and the ladder, but for the
rest of that day, whenever I appeared in the enclosure
round the cottage, the two swallows kept flying back-
wards and forwards low over my head, with shrill
cries of dislike and anger; so close did they pass over
my cap and with such menace that it was difficult to
avoid ducking the head. The next day I was wearing
a suit not so very different in colour, but with trousers
instead of knickerbockers. The swallows took no
notice of me. On the third day (Monday) I was again
wearing the knickerbocker suit; as soon as I appeared
outside the cottage, the persecution of me by the birds
began again and continued whenever I was near it.
On none of the days did the swallows take any notice

whatever of anyone else who came about the cottage or went in and out by the porch.

The episode struck me as an interesting example of discrimination by wild birds against a single person; and it was dependent entirely on clothes.

NOTE ON THE REAPPEARANCE OF

A PAIR OF TAME ROBINS

After the disappearance of the pair of robins in May 1926 six months passed without any sign of these or of any tame robin. In November a new robin beyond the further pond began to show signs of intelligence. Its territory was out of sight of the greenhouse and distant about 300 yards.

On 22nd November I started with the box of meal-worms in my pocket to continue the education of this bird, which was not yet hand-tame. I had just left the greenhouse, when a robin presented itself obtrusively and expectantly in the spiræa bush. The box was offered to it; the bird came at once on to my hand, stood there for some time eating meal-worms and occasionally warbling a challenge to another robin a little way off. It was very pleasant to feel once more, after an interval of six months, the confident clasp of the slender feet upon my fingers. The manners of this bird were precisely those of the male of the tame pair that had nested in this territory in the spring. Where had it been in the interval? Certainly not in this territory; for during August and up to this date in November I had from time to time tested every robin in this and adjoining territories by offering the meal-worm box. My advances had invariably been ignored, and when pressed had caused each bird to fly away. There was nothing in this day of November to make birds unusually hungry, and previous tame robins have, when present, accepted and asked for meal-worms daily from August onwards.

The conclusion is that this bird was the male of the tame pair, and that he had been absent since he was last seen in May.

Two days afterwards a robin presented itself on the yew in front of the greenhouse and snatched meal-worms one at a time from the box on my hand, precisely as the female of the tame pair had been used to do. But they were not paired now; the female after combat established her right to the greenhouse territory; the male had the adjoining territory to the west – a slope leading up to the house. He frequently followed me into the female's territory but was invariably routed; he would sometimes think the coast was clear when the female was inside the greenhouse. He would then sit on the yew hoping to be fed; but the female would espy him from within, and at once fly up and out through the trap ventilator and descend like a little fury and drive him back to his own place. Under these conditions they were fed separately and daily through the winter.

On 9th February the male was admitted to the greenhouse territory, and the two birds stood on the yew a few inches apart without fighting.

As the spring came on two other robins appeared, and there were combats in which four robins were sometimes engaged, and there was great confusion. At least one of the new birds was tamed, and I cannot be sure that the female did not change her mate. Not till April was she seen to be fed by the male.

All I can certainly say is that a pair of robins now (24th April 1927) have a nest in the same patch of ivy as last year on the kitchen-garden wall; the noise of the young when being fed is audible, and both parents come on the hand in the same manner as at this time last year.

I have used the terms 'male' and 'female' rather confidently, and it may be well to say that I have assumed the bird that sings persistently and that feeds the other to be the male, and that this has been the method of identification of sex.

Chapter XIII

Waterfowl

In 1921 I gave some account to a Naturalist Society of the collection of waterfowl at Fallodon. I thought it too technical and special to be of general interest, and I hesitated about reprinting it in a volume of collected addresses. It was, however, included, and judging from the reviews of the book,[1] the chapter on waterfowl was found to be more interesting than I had anticipated.

It is not intended to repeat here any of the substance

1 *Fallodon Papers.*

of that address; but more than five years have passed
since it was delivered, and it may be of interest to
give some account of incidents that have happened
and observations that have been made in these later
years.

It has been said that in species in which the drake
has no eclipse and the plumage of the two sexes is
alike, the drake assists in rearing the young brood.
Further experience has confirmed this. There was a
remarkable instance at Fallodon in 1926. A Chilian
teal nested some fifty yards away from the water in
the broad box edging of a flower bed. The nest was
close to a much-used garden path, but it was completely concealed by the box-leaves, which met above
it. The bird entered through a hole at the bottom of
the clipped box edging on the inner side. Seven eggs
were laid, and were hatched in May; both duck and
drake were always with the brood, the drake as
inseparable from and as devoted to the young birds
as was the duck. Four young ones were reared. I
succeeded, with the help of the parents, who were
pinioned birds and very tame, in training them to feed
from the hand, but they were left free, and no wing
was clipped or pinioned. When the young birds were
well on the wing in July, the duck was found to be
laying again in the same nest; she stripped a fresh lot
of down, the clutch was again seven eggs, and she
hatched them all, on the 5th August. The drake was

as attentive as before, this time six birds were reared; and not till they were well on the wing did the family break up.

It is, I imagine, rare for any wild duck to rear two broods in one season; and it could not happen in those species in which the drakes have an eclipse. Indeed, this incident is a remarkable example of the continued vigour, as well as the family affection of the drake Chilian teal. Any drake that had an eclipse would, by the end of May or early in June, have become dowdy, depressed and indifferent to his mate. The Chilian teal, on the contrary, remained as sprightly and gallant through the whole summer as he had been in the spring.

From this it would be reasonable to infer that it is an advantage to a species for the drake to have no eclipse. His care and attention must be an additional protection to the young brood and a help in keeping them together, and the season in which nesting is possible is prolonged. This theory, however, is not supported by the experience of our common wild duck. The mallard belongs to a large tribe of which there are many kinds, and some occur in every continent, including Australia. They seem to be all closely related. They are 'quack' ducks; the voice of the male, though much softer, is a 'quack' resembling that of the female. In this the mallard tribes differ from other kinds of ducks in which the note of the male has no resemblance whatever to that of the female. It is true that the male of our common wild duck in the ecstasy of courtship can utter a whistle, but this is not his usual note.

Mallards and their allied species have therefore something in common that distinguishes them from other species, such as wigeon, pintail and teal. In one respect, however, our common wild duck is an exception among others of its tribe. In most of these the sexes are alike in plumage throughout the year, and the drake has no eclipse. In our common species the eclipse is very marked. It comes upon the drake early in the summer, and the care of the young is left entirely to the duck. From this it would be reasonable to infer that our species would be at a disadvantage as compared with others of its group; that it would be less numerous. It is, on the contrary, the most widely distributed and thriving. If we consider the enormous numbers maintained by waterfowl that have an eclipse, such as wigeon, we are led to conclude that brilliant plumage, followed by eclipse, is no disadvantage; it may even be a positive advantage.

The vigour of the stock and the intelligence of our common wild duck are remarkable. They will come uninvited and unwelcome to the ponds at Fallodon. Beautiful as the drakes are in their season, they have a coarse appearance among the other kinds of waterfowl. The females especially are common and underbred in appearance and vulgar in manner. They are clever at finding the food that is meant for choicer birds, and their appetite is large. I endeavour, therefore, to exclude them. On one occasion a duck and her brood were captured, when the young were about a week old, and removed to a neighbour's lake at a safe distance. Two of the brood escaped the catching: they reared themselves, with no parent to guide them or to brood and cover them.

When my first waterfowl were bought in March 1884, it seemed to me no drawback that the birds were pinioned. My interest, like that of most collectors of waterfowl, was centred on variety of species, their plumage and their ways. Then came a wish to get the birds to nest, and great care was taken to rear the young: this was often done by taking the eggs away from the duck's nest and setting them under a bantam for greater security both in the nest and in subsequent protection of the young birds. In later years my point of view has changed; pinioned birds are no longer a complete satisfaction. It is not on humanitarian grounds that discontent has arisen: from all that I have seen and been told, it is evident that the pinioning of very young ducks does not cause suffering; they feed and show no sign of pain or discomfort after the operation, nor do they suffer appreciably in later life. Their plumage, health and spirits are good: it is no uncommon event for an unpinioned bird to pair year after year with the same pinioned mate; the two birds lead the same life together, and it cannot be much hardship to the pinioned bird to be compelled to remain in an enclosure in which the free bird stays voluntarily.

Nevertheless, pinioning is a blemish to the appearance, and more and more have my feeling and sentiment inclined to free birds. The pinioned bird is a prisoner: one cannot look at it and reflect that it stays by its own choice, that it remains by preference and not necessity. A guest once remarked to a great landowner on the promptness with which curtsies were dropped or hats touched by everyone they passed. 'Yes,' said the great man, 'they know very well that I *will* be popular on my own estate.' With pinioned birds there is a doubt as to the reason for their complacence: with free birds their tameness is a compliment.

I have therefore in recent years very greatly increased the proportion of free to pinioned birds at Fallodon, and by regular and patient attention on my part or on that of others when I am away from home, the standard of tameness has been raised to a very high plane. There may now be seen on the wing at Fallodon pintail, wigeon, tufted ducks, pochards, red-crested pochards, shovelers, Chilian pintail, Chilian teal, Chiloe wigeon, mandarins, and wood ducks (*Carolinus*). Of these free birds a considerable number, representing every one of the species named, except the shovelers, will come out of the water and take food confidently from the hand. In order to get this result many hours are spent, particularly in June, in taming brood after brood of young ducks: for it is when they are quite small that the training must be done. Even when the parent birds are tame, it often needs many days before their example and reassuring notes can overcome the innate suspicion that the little birds feel of a human hand.

The disadvantages of having rare waterfowl on these terms are serious. Numbers of them fly away and never return; many, no doubt, are shot; for no one, however well intentioned, can distinguish a rare duck when flight-shooting. The number of birds that disappear every season gives an uneasy feeling of spendthrift waste; for £5 or £6 is not an unusual price for a pair of the rarer species. The mere absence of the birds would not matter: the thought which hurts is that so many of them leave, not to be beautiful and interesting elsewhere, but to be shot unrecognised. It is seldom that I know definitely of the catastrophes, for none are ever shot on my own property. Two young Chiloe wigeon, both hand-tame, left me one October: they never returned, and in the following January the wing of a rare duck was sent to me for identification. It was the wing of a Chiloe wigeon in the plumage of its first year. The bird had been shot about twenty miles north of Fallodon. Chiloe wigeon in a free state are, I imagine, uncommon in Northumberland, and probably anywhere else in England, and there is little doubt that this wing was that of one of my young birds. Two points of interest attach to this occurrence. One is that the bird had not migrated and gone south, though it left me when the southward tide of migration was strong. As it is a South American species, its migratory instinct may well have been confused in the northern hemisphere. The second point is, that even in winter these young birds of a foreign species had been able to get food so easily that they never found it worthwhile to return to Fallodon to be fed, though they had remained within easy reach of it.

Another drawback incident to the freedom of the birds is that they settle for themselves the numbers of each species that are to remain with me; and as my accommodation in water is small,[1] there are too many birds of certain species. Tufted ducks are prone to what Peacock calls 'stay-at-homeativeness'. The young broods are apt to be content with the place in which they have been reared. The result is that day after day I have to look at a flotilla of twenty or thirty tufted ducks, sitting content, comfortable and secure on the limited space of water which all the other waterfowl

[1] There are only two ponds, and the larger is less than one acre in extent.

have to share. Most of the tufted ducks could well be spared and would be better bestowed elsewhere. Yet to interfere is impossible. Though they are all free birds, they could be caught by feeding them into a covered wire enclosure; but this catching would shock the whole collection, destroy their confidence, and undo in one fell moment the work of years spent in inducing the birds to believe that the place is safe and that mankind in this one spot can be trusted.

Some eight or ten of these tufted ducks will stand at my feet looking up in the most engaging way to be fed by hand: in the confusion of the catching, these, from which I should not wish to part, could not be distinguished from others that I should not miss. So the tufted ducks increase out of due proportion to the rest, and there is nothing to be done but to acquiesce. They must be well fed, too, for to stint them would be to stint other kinds, which are more rare and few in number and which it is desired to keep. One becomes positively servile in pampering free birds that one fears to lose.

In contrast with tufted ducks are pochards: these are very considerate and never take too great advantage of hospitality. Young pochards leave before the end of October; it is an exception when one of the young birds stays with me for the winter. Tameness makes no difference; however intimately tame a brood may be, the instinct to depart is the dominating influence.

Two pairs of free pochards have bred at Fallodon every season in the last two or three years. Of these, I think the females do not go away at all. The males leave when the females are sitting in May; this year (1926) one of them returned at the beginning of August, and the other about three weeks later. The first one could be identified with certainty, for he fed from the hand and had precisely the same manners as before he left. The second bird was not hand-tame, but would feed within a yard of me, and was evidently used to all the ways of the place: I assume, therefore, that he was one of the birds that had been here in the nesting season.

Pochards and tufted ducks do not seem to mate till after, and generally long after, the new year, whereas many wigeon, pintail, mandarins and wood-ducks come together soon after the eclipse is over, and court and go in pairs during the autumn; and thus have a longer period of domestic happiness. It is remarkable that male and female pochards should be so late in taking notice of each other, for the drakes have only a partial eclipse, much less marked than that of the other species with which they are here compared.

Every year I suffer the disadvantage and losses of having so many unpinioned waterfowl, but more and more the pleasure of having free birds tame preponderates.

To see a pair of Chiloe wigeon on the wing high in the air, conversing audibly as they fly, and to know that when they alight they will take food from the hand – all this is a satisfaction that no pinioned birds can give. To have even one such pair that stays is compensation for the loss of several that fly away and do not return.

In the last few years there have been many birds that by some individuality or ways of their own have become subjects of special interest. To each of these a little history belongs. One shall be selected as an example, both of the pleasure and the pain of having tame birds to which one becomes attached. I will call it the story of Elizabeth.

Elizabeth was a pintail; one of a brood reared in 1921 by an unpinioned mother that had paid the enclosure at Fallodon the compliment of nesting there. Several of the young pintails reared this year would take bits of bread from the fingers, but only three, one male and two females, would put their bills into the palm of the hand and thus eat their grain. These three birds continued to do this through the autumn and winter. In the spring of 1922 I lost track of them, and the male bird has not returned, or at any rate has not been identified again. But in the early autumn of 1922 the two females began to attend the evening feed regularly, and ate grain from the hand as before. One of them was rather darker in plumage than the other; in the spring of 1923 both disappeared again, and after the nesting season was over only one, the darker bird, presented itself and fed as usual. There were several other pintails, and they were all tame, but this was now the only one that ate corn from the hand: it became convenient now to have a name by which to speak of it, and thus it came to be called Elizabeth.

Elizabeth, when so disposed, would take food from the hand at any time and in any part of the grounds; but her favourite and regular place was to the right of the low bench from which the evening feed was given at the foot of a big larch. A root of the tree heaves up the ground almost level with this end of the bench, and here she would stand. If in the business of feeding the other birds her arrival was not noticed, she would make a little noise that sounded like gentle reproach: on turning my head I would see her standing there looking up at me expectant, till she was satisfied by a handful of grain held out to her. Every evening her presence was looked forward to, and if, as sometimes happened, she was absent for a day or two, there was a sense of disappointment and of something missing.

In spring the waterfowl do not attend the evening feed regularly: they are scattered and busy with nests; but in the spring of 1924 Elizabeth still came now and then, and it was evident from her manners that she had a nest and was sitting. A nest under a big thorn bush in a field some three hundred yards away was thought to be hers; but as there were other pintails sitting in the neighbourhood, there could be no certainty whose nest it was. It was robbed of all the eggs by vermin. Elizabeth never brought off a brood, and about the end of May she left. Not till November was she seen again, and then one evening there was the little note of reproach, and Elizabeth was standing in the usual place beside me. The unexpected return of a favourite bird after months of absence, during which it must have led a perfectly wild life and perhaps visited the Arctic zone, uplifts one with satisfaction. This year she remained as usual throughout the winter; but in the spring of 1925 she disappeared, presumably to nest elsewhere. Each season she had a mate, who would stand close by, but would not feed from the hand with her: whether it was the same drake every year was uncertain. This year she came back very early in the autumn, but in December she went away. It is a dangerous time, for there is much duck-shooting. One evening in January she reappeared at the evening feed in very sad case. She must have been able to fly, or she could not have come back over the fox-proof fence, and neither leg was broken; but both wings dragged, and she had a crouching walk. She put her bill in my hand, but seemed unable to swallow the corn in it and tried ineffectually to eat the grains that were scattered on the ground. The next evening she came once more, and this time I had some soaked bread ready for her. I gave her this by hand, and she ate a fair amount; but she was no better, and was never seen again.

It is impossible to have tame birds without facing these tragedies: one has to make up one's mind to do so, and to reflect that over a long series of years the tragedies are intermittent, whereas the interest given by the birds is a daily pleasure which is not only unflagging, but increases. Nevertheless the tragedy when it comes is very poignant. As to Elizabeth herself, the injury, whatever it was that befell her, must have been one that might happen to any pintail in a natural state; she was in her fifth year; that may be less than the average length of the life of a wild pintail; but for all the months of it spent at Fallodon, she had been more secure in severe weather from hardship such as scarcity of food, and less disturbed by fear and alarm, than wild birds of her kind: and for the rest, she had by going away at will been able to satisfy all the instincts for wild life.

Year after year there are like incidents of individual interest, of which the story of Elizabeth is but one example.

Chapter XIV

Waterfowl – *Continued*

In a collection of waterfowl peculiar satisfaction is given by the visit of wild birds. In May 1925 a pair of shovelers, both adults, arrived. At first they were wild and shy, and after a week or two the drake left, but the duck stayed on. In July two more shovelers came; from their size and plumage it was evident that they were young birds of the year; but they were wild, getting on the wing whenever anyone approached, and flying away to the other pond. One of these birds stayed and became tame. It was a small bird, but rather dark in colour, and eventually proved, as I expected, to be a drake. In the autumn and winter both these birds, the adult female and the young bird, grew quite tame, and would come close to be fed, either on water or land. They attended the evening feed regularly and ate grain as eagerly as any of the other waterfowl. This is a somewhat unexpected trait in wild shovelers, for dry corn is probably not their common food in a wild state, and their bills are ill-adapted for picking it up grain by grain from the ground. The young shoveler was especially confiding: he would feed close to my feet, but would not actually take bread from the hand: he would stare at a piece of bread held close to him, but would not eat it until it was dropped on the ground. It was not till after the new year that he began to show signs of male plumage; even then the change came very slowly and was not completed when he and the other wild shoveler went away in March. In September both birds returned, the male in eclipse. There was no doubt as to the identity of the male – he would again come close to my hand, stare at the piece of bread offered him, but refuse to take it till it was dropped on the ground. Shovelers have been hatched by a pinioned duck in recent years at Fallodon, but for at least fifteen years none have been reared. The two birds here described were therefore not birds bred on the place, and there is no reason to doubt that they were genuinely wild birds. They are both here now, at the end of January 1927, and the drake, who was so very late in coming into plumage in 1925, has now for over two months been in very bright and complete male colour. But he is still obstinate about taking food from the hand.[1]

Some part of the pleasure given by tame waterfowl is due to the reflection that many of them are by nature so exceedingly wild and distrustful of man. Mr J. G. Millais, in his valuable and magnificent volumes on British ducks, notes the very great difficulty of taming pintail and teal, and my experience agrees with his, except that I should say that teal were the more difficult. Only twice in forty-three years have pinioned teal nested at Fallodon.

Of pintails Mr Millais says: 'Even in confinement ... if whoever feeds them ceases to go near the pond for a few days, they seem to resume at once the instinctive fear of the wild state.' He says also: 'Pintails will never approach closely unless men are constantly around them, as in such public places as St James's Park and the Zoo.'

This is the character of birds caught wild and pinioned; but it is possible to rear a race of pintails that remain tame. Every autumn from six to a dozen come to the two ponds and remain till the spring. There are at least three pairs here now (January 1927).

[1] Both these shovelers left in February, and it will be interesting to see whether they return in the autumn to spend a third winter at Fallodon.

It happens that in 1925 and 1926 only one pair of pintails stayed to nest at Fallodon, and in each year the duck brought out her brood early in May in very inclement weather, and they all perished. No pintails have been reared at Fallodon since 1924, and the youngest birds among those now here must be at least in their third year. Every one of them has, for several months of each year, been absent, and led a perfectly wild life. When away they are probably as shy and distrustful of man as wild birds of their kind, but when again on the Fallodon ponds they are as tame as ever. Only one of those now wintering there will feed out of the hand, but they will all come to within six feet of me on land, and there feed and court and bicker with each other in a perfectly natural way. Long absences and wild life have not destroyed their confidence in a place that they have been brought up to believe to be safe. This instance of the pintails has been thought worth mentioning because of the reputation of the species for wildness. London provides examples on a large scale of waterfowl and gulls becoming tame in a place where they know that they are safe, but I have not myself seen pintails there behaving like tame birds; though others with better eyes and opportunities may have done so.

Tame as the Fallodon waterfowl have become – some of them will fly up and stand on the seat beside me to be fed – the wild instinct is always there. Any unusual movement upsets them: it does not do to knock out the ashes of a pipe against the seat when they are round it; and to put up a parasol in their presence causes disaster; on the other hand, one may put up a pair of binoculars without disturbing them, for they are used to this. The thumb may stroke the breast of a bird that is feeding out of the hand, but any attempt to stroke the back might never be forgiven. Their resentment of any unusual familiarity reminds me of the following story which my grandfather used to tell of Sydney Smith. In some party where he was present, one of the company had received and accepted an invitation to stay at Lambeth Palace. This man was somewhat forward in manner, and was talking with assurance and familiarity of his impending visit, though he had never been at Lambeth before. As they parted, Sydney Smith said to him, 'Let me give you one little bit of advice: when you get to Lambeth don't clap the Archbishop on the back and call him "Canterbury," because he isn't *used* to it.'

One disadvantage of having pinioned birds is that hybrids will sometimes occur. One cannot always ensure that every pinioned bird has a mate; pairs are broken by one bird dying or meeting with mishap, and with rare kinds the loss cannot always be replaced at once. This leads to *mésalliances*. They are not very common, and when they occur nature takes care that the offence is not perpetuated. I have noticed that hybrid drakes, the offspring of two kinds not closely related, have no clear voice, nothing but a sort of husky whisper.

Closely related birds of the mallard species will produce any number of fertile and ugly mongrels. I have, however, had experience of one hybrid among other kinds which has been sufficiently interesting to merit some attention.

In 1917 a male pinioned white-eyed pochard paired with a pinioned mate of his own species, and, as far as could be observed, was faithful to her in the early part of the season: but when she had been sitting on eggs for some time, he courted an unpinioned tufted duck; he swam with this bird, sat by her on the bank, and consorted with her all day; she in time nested, and reared two birds of her brood. They were left free, and proved to be a drake and a duck; they paired and went away together for a while in the autumn; but returned, and though occasionally absent, made the enclosure their home. They did not breed in 1918, but the female nested in 1919, and that year and every year since she has nested and brought a brood to the water; the younger generations have also been fertile, for though most of them have gone permanently into wildlife, there were at least three nests of these hybrids last year (1926) at Fallodon. The broods are as numerous and as vigorous as tufted ducks. These hybrids have so far paired entirely with each other, and they breed true to type. Each generation resembles the first pair. The original male has had the peculiarity that he will not touch bread: he will look on while the other birds eat it; but however close to him a piece falls in the water he will not take the trouble to pick it up. No other of my tame waterfowl is so uniformly disdainful, and it is by this habit that I have been able to identify him. The female was not an exception in this way, and it is not therefore certain that it is the original female with which the drake still pairs; but I have assumed that this is probable, and that she is one of the hybrids that have nested every year. Both sexes show very conspicuously the white underparts at the end of the body that is characteristic of white-eyed pochards; the females have the dark eye of a female white-eyed pochard, but the plumage is not so rufous and they are larger birds. The males have eyes distinctly paler than those of a tufted drake, and they have no tuft on the head. On each side, when in plumage, they have a panel corresponding to the white panels of tufted drakes; but in the hybrids this is a soft grey. The black on the head in sunlight has a green instead of the violet sheen of a tufted drake. The drake hybrids have a complete eclipse. The notes, so far as I have been able to observe, are not like those of tufted ducks, but very closely resemble those of white-eyed pochards. So far these hybrids exhibit the characteristics of a separate and permanent species.

There are other pleasures in watching waterfowl

besides that of attention to individual birds or species. Wordsworth in 'To a Highland Girl' notes the precious power of memory to preserve a vision of beauty or the impression of the mood that accompanied it. I will try to describe one such scene, as memory recalls it.

It was Christmas morning, many years ago when my sight was less impaired; the sun does not rise till after half past eight in Northumberland at this season. I went out after breakfast; the waterfowl had been fed rather later than usual: they were still finishing their meal under the big larch tree or were assembled at this end of the pond, which, being much shut in by trees and shrubs, was still in dark shadow. I went to the other pond some two hundred yards away and sat on the garden seat on the farther side. This pond is more open: there are no tall trees on the east side, and all the water was in full sunlight. There was not a bird on it; there was no stir in the air; the surface of the water was smooth and without motion. Presently pintail, wigeon, tufted ducks, pochards and one or two other kinds began to come flying over the intervening shrubs and trees from the pond where they had been fed. They came, some singly, some two or three together. None of them had yet seen the sun that morning, and each and all, as if in greeting to it, began to sport and play. They threw the water over their bodies, they raised themselves up on it and flapped their wings: they swam rapidly about in all directions, low in the water with quick and eager forward dartings of the head and neck. They sprang from the water into the air and took headers from the air into the water; they made short flights in one direction, lit on the water for a moment, and made another flight back in the direction whence they came; they dived unexpectedly, travelled underwater, came up in some new place, and then, as if surprised at what they saw, dived again with exceeding suddenness. They splashed for the sake of splashing; there was not a square foot of water that was not in constant agitation. For some time the scene was one of motions of delight and exhilaration. At length first one bird and then another flew up on to the bank that faced the sun, or on to the south end of a little island; there they stood or sat, many of them side by side in pairs, and rested motionless or slept. Some half-dozen birds only remained on the water, and each of these was still, the head turned round and the bill resting in the feathers of the back. All was quiet; there was no sound or stir; the water was again smooth, the reflections in it were composed once more; the sun still shone; on the water and the birds; on the scarlet-barked willows and the delicate bareness of winter trees on the opposite side. Anyone who had come upon it now might have thought that the place was under some spell. He would have seen the man on the seat sit motionless, too, for a long time; entranced rather than asleep: the scene had indeed sunk down into his heart and 'held it like a dream'. There are times when man's consciousness seems laid to rest in some great whole, of which he has become a part. There are hours of which it can be said, 'Thought was not: in enjoyment it expired.' So it was now, and if anything stirred in the mind at all, it was an echo of the words, 'And God saw that it was good.'

Conclusion

Anyone who reads this book will necessarily be struck by its incompleteness. There is little or no mention of birds of prey, of sea and shore birds, of bitterns, bearded tits and the wonderful and fascinating bird life of the Norfolk Broads. This is not because the interest of the things omitted is depreciated or under-valued; the omissions occur because the purpose of the book is to deal only with those aspects of bird life that have happened to be a most constant source of interest and pleasure to the author and to have come most frequently under his observation. Even within this limited scope there are many things that have not been included. For instance, little has been said of that very attractive race of common birds – the wagtails, especially the grey wagtail, which in its plumage and ways is one of the most delicately beautiful of our birds. To keep the book within easily read compass, no attempt has been made to give a complete account of any bird, and very little use has been made of other books in order to supplement my own fragmentary knowledge.

Here and there questions are asked or problems stated: I am conscious that in a wider range of reading than my own there may be found answers to these questions and solutions of these problems which have not come under my notice. These shortcomings may be open to criticism; but this criticism may spread more widely the knowledge that experts already possess, and the shortcomings of the book may thus serve a useful purpose.

I will end with some general reflections.

Most people who study nature have the impulse to look for some general laws that will account for the life and growth and manifestations that they see about them. A great astronomer (I think it was Kepler) is reputed to have said, when discovering some law governing the motions of the stars, that he was thinking God's thoughts after Him. In like manner one who believes in a divine creator seeks to discover principles and laws that regulate life and growth; in doing so he feels that he is understanding something of the plan or procedure of supreme intelligence. But the materialist also has the same impulse to search for law in nature. He may be unwilling to accept the hypothesis of conscious creative intelligence, yet chaos is repulsive to him; he therefore searches for some orderly even if it be a blind process to account for what he sees. Thus people of all creeds or no creed are drawn to the search for laws and guiding principles in nature. They seek to find rest in theories of evolution, survival of the fittest, natural selection and so forth. In birds, for instance, it is very satisfactory to find and note some habit, or some protective colouring of plumage or eggs, that has been evolved and to which the survival and welfare of the species is due. Yet it seems to be beyond the utmost ingenuity of human intellect to stretch any of these natural laws or processes sufficiently to make them cover and account for all that we see. I have therefore taken refuge in the hypothesis that there is in nature some tendency or purpose ever at work for the sake of creating infinite variety. Much of this appeals to man in the form of what he calls beauty. In civilised mankind, at any rate from Homer onwards, the sense of natural beauty has been as innate as the moral sense of right and wrong. People will decide, each for himself, whether these senses are a particle of the Divine innate in mankind[1] or whether they are a blind outcome of man's experience, evolved by survival of the fittest. I will not digress further into this vast subject. Personally I find satisfaction in the comprehensive though vague conception that infinite variety is part of the purpose or plan in nature; and that within this larger conception there are others, such as protective colouring, that do effective work but produce more limited results.

The moral being of man, however, stands outside and apart from the wildlife of Nature. It is just because this wildlife is amoral, not troubled by questions of right and wrong, that we find it so refreshing and restful.

Some years ago there was published a book about birds which gave the impression that the author definitely and deliberately preferred birds to men. There was in it a hint of a comparison between birds and men that was unfavourable to humanity; this was distasteful. I did not indeed feel disposed to take sides in the comparison, nor was I provoked to any indignation by the author's preference; but I felt the comparison to be entirely out of place. Mankind is so separate from the wildlife of nature that the two things

[1] Wordsworth expresses this in a fine and very strong passage in *The Excursion*, book 4, lines 32–65. The passage is too long to quote, but it is very relevant.

are not comparable at all. Man's highest concern individually and collectively is with moral problems, with right and wrong. If he imports these considerations into the study of wild birds and animals, he will distort the truth of what he sees. The wild creatures act admirably according to the inherited instinct of their kind, but they are not troubled by sense of virtue or of shame. Therefore it is that the study of their life is such a recreation to man; it opens a door through which self-consciousness escapes and leaves him free for a time from moral doubts and strivings.

But though self-consciousness is in abeyance while watching wildlife, the restfulness that we feel is not dull, insensate quiescence: interest is aroused and may be quickened to the point of excitement by what we see. We are keenly alive and yet remain free from all anxiety about success or failure, from shyness, embarrassment or any concern that is personal to ourselves.

The watching of wild animals or birds gives yet another pleasure, that of a sense of privilege. We see many things that as a rule are concealed from men's eyes. The presence of man causes fear and suspicion in wild creatures; they flee or they hide. We may walk through a wood and see very little of the wildlife that is in it. We shall see or hear something of small birds that are used to man; one or more flustered woodpigeon may be heard taking flight, and a rabbit here and there may bolt in fear to its burrow. We see these wood-pigeons and rabbits for an instant, and no more. But numbers of creatures that we do not see have noted our approach, their eyes are watching us. Alarm has been communicated by one to another, and much of the wildlife about us is in suspense while we walk past. If we sit down in some secluded spot, unobtrusive and still, we shall presently understand how much there is that as passers-by we never see. In no long time the wild creatures will forget that there is a human presence or will become reassured as to our intentions. One who thus watches may hear a pattering coming towards him on the fallen leaves, and if he does not stir, a squirrel may go up the trunk of the very tree at the foot of which he is sitting, he will hear the tick of its sharp claws on the rough bark as it ascends. A rabbit will appear, nibble and move on leisurely. A questing hedgehog will pass slowly close to him, stopping now and then to investigate something with its sharp little snout. It is in such circumstances too that something rare may be seen; as once happened when I was eating my lunch under a big yew tree and a hawfinch, a bird very seldom seen at Fallodon, came and made its meal of yew berries within a few feet of my head. If the season be spring, birds carrying food or building material will go to and from their nests. In all this one who sits and watches has the feeling of a privileged spectator.

It is with the aspect of nature as solace, recreation and delight that this book has been concerned. It is good to be alone with nature sometimes; to men like W. H. Hudson, it is essential, if they are ever to express what they have it in them to give.

There is, however, a higher effect of natural beauty upon man; it is especially wrought upon him by the inanimate aspects of nature, light upon water, 'the unnumbered smiling of the sea,' 'the fresh earth in new leaves drest,' 'the light of setting suns'; tributes to it are paid by great poets in all ages. There is a unique sense of security about this beauty. In places, some of it may be marred by man's work, but in its large aspects it is indestructible by human agency: it is also not a private possession, and thus neither cause of envy to others nor source of anxiety to those who enjoy it. It leads to high thoughts.

Wordsworth says that one impulse from a vernal wood can teach us more, than all the sages, of man and of moral good and evil. In this he says what by his own experience he knew to be firm truth. A modern simile may help to explain what is meant. We are told that from a height in an aeroplane the physical eye can see deeper down into water; that even on land it can trace markings on the open ground that are not perceptible to one standing on the surface. So when feeling is raised to an unusual height by contemplation of natural beauty, by something that quickens while it soothes and calms, the mental and moral perceptions may penetrate more deeply 'into the life of things'.

This is high matter, beyond the scope of this book. It is nature as inspiration; some great minds have felt it so in all ages, but they have found it in largest measure not by watching the life of wild creatures, but by contemplating the beauty and splendour of that part of creation which for the sake of a distinction we call inanimate nature.

Pleasure in Nature

An address given to the School Nature Union,
by Edward Grey in London, on 2nd January 1923.

The subject on which I have undertaken to say something is important for all persons who are concerned about education, yet it is a somewhat difficult one to approach from the point of view of teaching. The subject I have taken is that of 'Pleasure in Outdoor Nature'. Now, given that a teacher is capable and a pupil is willing, you can make sure of teaching knowledge. You can impart knowledge, but you cannot make sure of imparting pleasure. In order to illustrate what I mean I will mention the game of golf. Anybody can be taught the rules of the game of golf and how to play golf. One person may turn out to be a very good player and another an indifferent player, yet even an indifferent player may find so much pleasure in the game that it becomes an enthusiasm and a passion. But in the case of another person with equal aptitude for the game, though you can make certain of teaching him the rules and how to play, you may find that, instead of imparting pleasure, the more he knows the more bored he gets, and he leaves it off. Thus you can make a certainty of imparting knowledge, but pleasure you cannot impart, unless there is in the person taught some natural aptitude and capacity for enjoyment. Nevertheless, the imparting of pleasure, it seems to me, is a very important part of education. There is a great deal of discontent in the world; some is due to poverty, to ill-health, to want of leisure, to overwork, to unhappy outward circumstances; moralists would say that much of it is due to the fact that people have not sufficient moral basis, to which an American girl is said to have retorted, 'No doubt people who are good are happy, but they do not have a good time.' That sort of discontent with which the moralist or economist has to deal is outside my subject. The proposition I would put to you is this, that people, who have a reasonable amount of leisure, should have a habit of spending that leisure and a capacity for spending it in a way that brings interest and pleasure, and that this is a great factor in making life contented. That is the proposition. For this purpose, if you can impart the power of taking real pleasure in the best poetry and the best literature, no doubt you will have given the most easily accessible and most permanent and lasting form of making leisure satisfactory; because books, even the best, are easily accessible, and all that is necessary for the enjoyment of them is that you should, in fine weather, find some quiet spot out of doors, or that you should have access to a room in which there is no telephone.

Books I would put first. By books I mean the power of taking pleasure in the best literature. But next to books I would put the capacity for finding pleasure in outdoor nature. There are two great advantages in it; two great qualities that belong to it. One is that it means a capacity for taking pleasure in common things. The beauty of the world and the interesting things in wild nature are there for everybody to enjoy, and the fact that one person enjoys them does not diminish the power of others to enjoy them provided only that everybody, who takes pleasure in outdoor nature, will observe the one simple rule, which is far too often broken, that you should take your pleasure in outdoor nature without destroying or disturbing. As long as you do that, your pleasure is not diminishing anyone else's pleasure. For instance, supposing you are in one of the London parks, and there happens to be, as happily there often is, a thrush or blackbird singing, and you stop to enjoy the song, the fact that someone else stops to enjoy it does not diminish your pleasure, it increases it; but if someone throws a stone at the bird, he destroys your pleasure.

The other quality is that the best kind of pleasure in outdoor nature does not depend on novelty, but upon enjoying things which recur in the seasons of the year. Every season of the year brings its own aspects of beauty or its own subjects of interest. They recur year after year; it is precisely because of this that they become increasingly familiar, and we look forward to them every year. If you wish to cultivate pleasure, there are three parts of it to be cultivated. One is anticipation, another realisation, and the third is retrospect. You can only have perfect anticipation of pleasure if it is a pleasure you have enjoyed before, so that you know before it arrives exactly what it is like and the sort of feeling you are going to get. outdoor nature has a succession of seasons and every year they bring round the same procession of beauty and interest. I am going to illustrate these general propositions from the study of birds, but please do not think I am going to give instruction to you about birds. My own knowledge is not that of an expert. Like many people who have been at the mercy of public life, which is a very tyrannous affair, I have passed the age of sixty and still have such deficiency of information that I am not really capable of giving instruction about anything.

What I would like to try to convey to you, having had much pleasure myself in the observation of birds, is that you can get pleasure from observing them. The word 'consider' is used in the Bible in just the sense that applies to watching objects in nature; the sense of giving attention in order to appreciate and admire. 'Hast thou *considered* my servant, Job?' '*Consider* the lilies of the field.' I want this afternoon to *consider* certain birds and certain aspects of them in order that we may understand, appreciate, and admire them. Of course there are some people who take no pleasure in birds; they have not the capacity for doing so. But it is known to everybody that to a large number of people birds are a source of very great interest and pleasure. Why is this so? Because they have certain remarkable and attractive natural qualities. First of all, there is the power of flight, in itself a thing worth considering. The flight of different species of birds, the manner of their flying, differs so that an expert can tell by the manner of a bird's flight what species of bird it is. There are, amongst our common birds, all sorts and manners and ways of flying, from the buoyant and prolonged flight of the common gulls down to the rising and falling flight of the woodpeckers, which seems to be so precarious that you doubt sometimes whether the woodpecker will be able to fly to the next tree. On the other hand, if you will lie on your back on a fine day, you may see gulls sailing high in the air, without apparent effort or movement of wing, as though it was not necessary for them to descend at all; and between these two, the apparently inexhaustible power of the gull to sustain itself in the air, and the rising and falling flight of the woodpecker whose wings are weak – between these there are all sorts and degrees of the power of flight, and from that point of view alone our common birds become of interest.

The next aspect of birds is their plumage and wonderful variety of colouring which presents all sorts of questions to which I can give you no answer. Why should males, for instance, have a bright colour and females a comparatively dull colour, as in the case of the chaffinch and bullfinch; while in other cases, for instance, the hedge sparrow (which I prefer to call the dunnock because it has nothing to do with the sparrow), both the males and females are of the same colour? And then you have a further variety of plumage when you come to the common wild duck, of which the drake is for the greater part of the year a very brilliant bird with most beautiful colours and the female is sober-coloured. But when the female is nesting the male bird, the drake, undergoes a change; he loses all that bright colour and becomes a shabby and dowdy object, and, as if ashamed of himself, slinks out of sight, so that, when the duck comes on the water with her brood of young ducklings, the drake has disappeared. There are other waterfowl, especially some foreign ones, some of them very nearly related to our own common wild duck, which have an entirely different plan as regards plumage. In some the male is brilliant, but the female is also brilliant, and where that is the case the male bird is allowed to retain the brilliancy of his colour all the year round. In other cases the male bird is sober-coloured like the female and he retains the same colour all the year round. And there is this curious accompaniment of this variety of habit, so far as I have been able to observe, where the drake remains. the same colour as the female throughout the year, whether brilliant or sober-coloured; when the female has hatched her brood of young ducklings, the drake helps to tend and bring them up, whereas our own wild drake and other drakes, which are brilliant at one time, but dull at another, do not go with the young brood at all to help to bring them up. Why this is so I cannot say, but it is a matter of interest to find in some species of birds males brilliant and females sober-coloured, in other species both sexes sober-coloured, in others both sexes brilliant-coloured, as, for instance, the kingfisher, and in some species the male brilliant-coloured for only one part of the year and sober-coloured for the other part. The reasons for all these different arrangements in the plumage of different species are subjects of speculation.

The third aspect of birds I would take is the fact that they lay eggs of such various colours and build nests of such various shapes and substance. If I had to give a prize for nest building amongst our common birds I would give it to the long-tailed tit, which is a bird distributed over the whole of Great Britain. You meet with it frequently, from Sutherland to the South of England, in every county where I have been and where there is anything like a reasonable amount of plantation. It builds a most elaborate nest, and the whole time taken for the building of the nest, the hatching of the eggs, and the fledging of the young is a very long one – much longer than in the case of any other British bird I know.

When I was in office I had a cottage in the country to which I went at weekends, and one Sunday morning before the middle of March I observed from the window a pair of long-tailed tits building their nest in a sweetbriar hedge. When I went out and looked at the nest it was then like an ordinary nest, cup-shaped. A long-tailed tit is not content with that, but it builds a nest like a bag with a hole near the top. Every week

I went down there the building and business of the
nest was going on. It so happened that the 19th May
that year was a Sunday and I was at my cottage. It
also happened that this particular day, about noon,
was the time when the young birds first came out of
the nest. It also happened that I was standing close
by the nest at the time when the little birds first came
out of it. Thus you will see that this pair of long-
tailed tits required about two months and a half from
the time they began to build their nest to the time the
young came out of it. During all those weeks, when I
could be there, the nest was a subject of interest to
me, and many of you living in the country may have
the same experience provided that you will yourselves,
and are able to induce other people, to observe the
rule not to disturb or destroy.

Long-tailed tits are particularly interesting from
another point of view. The birds go in a company
and the brood remains together all the autumn and
winter, but early in March you will see the long-tailed
tits in pairs, and if you will look closely you will see
about that time that they have some little nesting
material in their beaks, and if you watch them you
will see them going to the nest and you can locate it.
Sometimes it is rather high up in the fork of a tree,
generally oak or ash, but as often as not it is only
four or five feet from the ground in a gorse bush or
an ordinary hedge. Whether they think they are so

small that you do not see them or whether they are so intensely busy in their work, it so happens that they are not at all shy, and you can stand at a distance of three yards from the nest quite openly and watch them build. You will see first one bird and then the other get into the nest when it is in cup shape and make it round and smooth by rubbing its breast round and round against the wall of the nest. You will see it arch its head over the sides of the nest and pull some of the outside over and inwards, weaving it thus; and when the nest is completed outside, the birds will line the inside with feathers. Then if you like you can help in the building of the nest. If you can collect small feathers and put them close to the nest, you can stand near and see the long-tailed tits take the feathers that you put for them and use them in their nest building. When the young birds have fledged you can, without doing any harm, take the nest and examine it, because I have never known long-tailed tits use their nest a second time. I have been told that the feathers used in the lining of a long-tailed tit's nest have been counted to number more than nine hundred. That seems incredible; I have not verified it, but any of you can do so.

It does not do to take every nest after the birds are fledged, because some of them are used again. I have known a blackbird rear two successive broods in the same season in the same nest, and after that a pair of pied wagtails took the nest, made a new cup in it, and reared their young in it.

Next let us take an instance of a bird which builds not only one nest, but more than one. The common wren often builds more nests than are used for eggs. The nest that is used for eggs is lined with feathers, but one or more nests are often built apparently with equal skill, except that they are not lined with feathers, and have no eggs put into them. These nests are often referred to as 'unoccupied dwellings,' but it is not an accurate description. I found one of these nests near my house one summer, and in the autumn and winter I used occasionally to go after sunset and look at the nest, and whenever I went a single wren came out of it. So it was quite clear that that particular nest, though not built for eggs, was used by a wren as a bedroom through the autumn and winter, though I cannot be sure whether it was the same wren that built the nest.

Next I come to a less cheerful subject in the way of nests. If you study the habits of birds, you will find at one end of the scale what I would call the creditable and at the other end the discreditable aspect of a habit, and at the discreditable end you will generally find the cuckoo. Please do not think that I do not like cuckoos. I am very fond of them, but I can only defend my liking for cuckoos in the way that I have heard some people defend their liking for a somewhat disagreeable friend. They usually say, 'I cannot help liking him, I know him so well.' As you know, the cuckoo has no nest of its own. It uses other birds' nests; it does not sit on its own eggs, and the young cuckoo turns the other birds out of the nest. Some thirty years ago, when I was in office, I found at one weekend a dunnock's nest with a cuckoo's egg among those that the dunnock had laid. Close by I found a whitethroat's nest with eggs. I came down at the end of the following week and visited both nests to see how they were getting on. In the dunnock's nest there was lying there at the bottom, a young cuckoo, alone, naked, blind, hideous, and apparently helpless. I then went to look at the whitethroat's nest, and found that there were recently hatched young birds in number corresponding with the eggs I had seen there a week before. I borrowed, temporarily, one of the little birds from that nest and put it in the dunnock's nest with the little cuckoo, and saw that apparently helpless hideous thing turn the little whitethroat out of the nest. You can try this for yourselves; and if you cannot find a newly hatched bird to put in with the cuckoo, you can induce the cuckoo to perform by making a small piece of wool into a ball, very lightly and loosely made, about the size of a recently hatched little bird. You can now see the cuckoo's methods of procedure exhibited on a film, and the experiment I have mentioned can be made by anybody who can find a young cuckoo in a nest: then you can watch it repeat the performance for yourselves; you can do this, provided you use a certain amount of tact and care, without disturbing either nest, and without injury to any of the objects on which you are experimenting.

A further aspect of birds, perhaps the most attractive of all, is the gift that some of them have of song. If people wish to appreciate our common birds, they must learn their songs. There is more pleasure to those who know them in the songs of birds than in almost any other aspect of bird life. It takes some trouble to learn the songs, but it is almost essential to pleasure in bird life to have a reasonably good knowledge of bird songs. The best time to get this knowledge is from the middle of April to the middle of May, when all the birds are in full song, when the summer birds are here or are on the way to us, and the leaves are not fully open on all the trees, so that you get the best view of the birds. The songs of our common birds are no doubt known to many of you, and I would only say one or two things about them. First of all, if you are fond of songs of birds, make a point of not letting any single month of the year go by without hearing the robins and the wrens sing, because these two birds can be heard every month in the year. If there is a very cold and severe month you, may not be able to hear them, but in any average year you can hear them sing in every month. And the wren's song is remarkable for its exceeding loudness compared with the size of the bird. You will not have much difficulty in getting close to the wren, when it is singing, and if you consider the smallness of its body, the loudness of its song, the vehemence of it and the animation of the body, well, really, I have sometimes been afraid that the little body would burst and be shattered by the vehemence of the song. These two birds you can hear sing in every month of the year, but there are other birds that sing only for a few months.

The blackbird is one of our best singers, but you will not, as a rule, hear much of its song before March or after the month of June. I have known of people hearing blackbirds in the month of January, but when I have been able to investigate the matter, I have found a missel thrush to be the bird they had heard singing. In the early part of the year the hearing of the first blackbird's song is a thing specially to look forward to, precisely because you have not heard it for so long. This is an instance where anticipation increases pleasure. And then, as the season goes on, there come the summer birds which have spent the winter in North Africa or even farther south. There is not only pleasure in hearing their songs each spring for the first time, but there is something romantic in thinking of the immenseness of the journey they may have accomplished since you heard them the year before. A swallow, ringed in this country in the summer, has, I am told, been found as far south as Natal, thousands of miles away, yet, if all went well, that swallow would have returned to this country, and to the particular spot in this country, where it had been reared. And so with other birds.

The anticipation in the spring of the coming of these birds from the places where they have spent the winter, is a thing to which one looks forward with the greatest interest. You will probably hear the first blackcap, the first willow-warbler, and the first wood-warbler, and so forth each year in much the same place as you heard it before, and so, when one gets fond of these birds and gets the habit of listening for them in the same place at the same time every spring, the satisfaction of having your anticipation realised, of hearing the same song in the same place for perhaps thirty years, and knowing that same bird or its successor has come back to the same spot, is a satisfaction which gives us peculiar pleasure.

It is not only of the birds which come to us in the summer that I would say something. There is also the other migration to look forward to, the birds which come to us from farther north or farther east to spend the winter in this country. One familiar instance is the woodcock. Many woodcocks breed in this country, and presumably never leave these islands. But the great majority of the woodcocks we have in the autumn and winter come from farther north or farther east. They cross the North Sea. The North Sea is a formidable width for small birds to cross. We are told by those who have studied these things that there was a time when the North Sea was all land, and perhaps that is the reason why some birds undertake this tremendous journey across the North Sea. If the species came that way when the North Sea did not exist, I suppose they may have kept up the habit when the North Sea was gradually formed, though I am not sure whether birds existed at the time when there was no North Sea.

I was once lying on the sand hills by the shore in Northumberland on a fine, bright, still day about the end of November. I was lying on my back looking up at the sky and I saw a woodcock arrive evidently from a great height with great velocity behind its descent. It slanted down over me at tremendous speed. It descended with wings rigid, not quite fully expanded; it seemed to come with precipitate and great speed from very high up. It lit in the rough grass about seventy yards behind me. I wished to know if it was tired after its long flight, so I went to see how it was. It rose several yards in front of me and flew away over the fields inland with no sign of being tired, and from that I judged that in the ordinary way, with fine weather, birds can cross the North Sea quite easily without being exhausted or tired. When they meet with bad weather they arrive very exhausted and no doubt many perish on the way.

However, it is not very surprising that the woodcock crosses the North Sea, when the smallest bird we have, the golden-crested wren, crosses it in numbers every autumn. The golden-crested wren is very common in this country wherever there is woodland, especially fir trees. If you get to know their song you can realise how common they are. Many of them breed in this country and probably never leave it. They are not very shy; you can get close to them, and the only difficulty in watching them is that they are so very restless. Now the next time you have the opportunity of getting close to one, just consider the fact that, though that particular bird may never have crossed the North Sea, thousands and thousands of golden-crested wrens exactly like it, as small and apparently as weak, do cross the North Sea every year. One observer in Heligoland years ago, in 1882, saw such a mass of golden-crested wrens arriving over the sea that he compared them to a snowstorm, every bird representing a flake.

One more instance I would give you as to migration, to show you how attractive it may be and to show you also how much can be done in taming birds. In 1921, in my garden, there were reared two or three broods of wigeon, which, as you know, is a British duck. There are some that breed in Scotland, but the bulk of them go much farther north to breed and come to us in flocks in autumn and winter. Three of these birds reared in the garden grew so tame that they would take food out of my hand, not snatching it, but continuing to feed with the bill in the palm of my hand with complete confidence, though in a wild state wigeon are very shy birds. Last spring they went away – two drakes and one duck. Presumably they joined flocks of wild wigeon going north. They may not have gone far or they may have gone very far north; anyhow, they were away for about seven months. In November of this year the female bird came back, and came up to me and began feeding in exactly the same way out of my hand as she had done before she went away. About three weeks afterwards one of the male birds came back and did exactly the same. It is exceedingly attractive if you can make birds tame so that, although they may be away amongst wild birds six or seven months, they yet come back to the same place, and are as tame as they were before.

Birds have to a greater degree, I think, than any other animate creature, except man, the power to express joy. I will give one or two instances. The flight and song of the lark are familiar to you; it is a real and evident joy flight. The note of the curlew in spring is a long, vibrating whistle, which is full of joy and very wonderful in expression; this is uttered mainly in the air, but sometimes partly on the ground. The snipe, too, has a joy flight; it flies in a wide circuit and, making a short descent from time to time in the air, achieves with the vibration of its tail feathers a noise like the bleating of a goat, which apparently gives the snipe great satisfaction. It will fly round and round for some time continually making that noise, and you cannot watch it without seeing that the flight is an expression of joy.

You have also the family life of birds to consider. Nearly all our British birds are monogamous. There are some exceptions. The black cock – black game – which are indigenous British birds, are polygamous. I do not count the pheasant because the pheasant is not an indigenous bird. He was imported from the East and brought his Eastern customs with him. But most of our birds – the vast majority – are monogamous, and the larger birds – perhaps the smaller ones too – pair for life. I warned you before that when you studied the habits of birds you always found the cuckoo at the discreditable end, and the cuckoo is said to be polyandrous. Though with very few exceptions our birds are all monogamous, in family life they differ. The long-tailed tit's family remain together all through the autumn and winter, sometimes joined by another family. Rooks, of course, live in a community. I think it is not so much family life as life of a community in the case of adult rooks, but with long-tailed tits and partridges it is a real family life which is continued after the young birds have grown up until pairing time in the next year. Anybody who has had a tame covey of partridges knows how attractive their family life is. The difficulty I have found is that they have never stayed with me after October, they have fallen in with wild birds and left the garden, but a tame covey of partridges, while it remains, is one of the most attractive things I know. That is a high form of family life.

Now consider the robin. He has as little family life as he can. Of course a pair of robins rear their brood each year; they may even have a second brood, but when the young are able to look after themselves the old birds make the young ones separate from them. And they are not content with that, but the male and female will not spend the autumn and winter together, but each robin has its own territory in which it remains separate and alone through the autumn and winter. If you work in the woods or in the garden you will notice that you are often attended by a robin, but only one at a time, and if another turns up there is a fight between the two. The law of robins apparently is that, except in the actual nesting period, each robin must have one territory, and if another robin comes he or she is breaking the law of robins. This law is as unalterable as that of the Medes and Persians; it is probably much older and it has certainly lasted much longer. I know of a robin in the nesting season that was so anxious to get food for its young that it acquired a habit of coming on a human hand to get food. It reared two broods this year, and for a time the young were in the same place with it. This robin remains there now and he will come on the hand and sit there and feed, he is so confident. But he never follows you from his own particular territory; if you want to give him food, you must go to his territory. If you go to another part of the garden some fifty yards away, another robin will come and stand by you, and if you put your hand on the ground he or she (whichever it is) will take something out of your hand. Its habits are quite different from those of the other robin. You never see the two together.

Then again I pass to the discreditable end of the scale and find the cuckoo, which has no family life at all. It is sometimes said that cuckoos exercise a certain kind of superintendence over their young that are reared by other birds; but this is doubtful.

I have taken these instances of birds from common things, because I am trying to show you the sort of pleasure in bird life which anybody that has an interest in birds may find. All the things I have been telling (except the instance of the wigeon, which I admit requires an enclosure with a pond, where things can be kept quiet) are what anybody who lives in the country may notice and enjoy for himself; and they cost nothing. You want really nothing except the power of walking about, good eyesight, and good hearing. Of course, a push bicycle is very useful, far better than a motor bicycle or a motor car, which ties you to the roads and makes speed the main object. A push bicycle is a much more subservient thing. It is silent, and it can be wheeled across places where no motor can be taken. A good pair of field glasses are also useful.

One can go on talking for ever about what has been seen and observed, and it is open to everybody to multiply observations for themselves of things that are within their reach. To tell them is the best way of imparting to, or implanting in, other people something of the pleasure that one has got one's self in bird life or in outdoor nature. Of course, outdoor nature includes many other things about which I am not qualified to speak. Sir Frederick Keeble, I have no doubt, could tell you the enormous difference it makes in life to take pleasure in wild flowers and have knowledge of them. I have not got that knowledge, but a friend told me the other day that when bicycling near my home with an ordinary hedge on either side of the road, and a wood on part of one side of it, in one half-mile without getting off his bicycle, he counted forty-six different kinds of wild flowers. Think what that half-mile was, from the point of view of interest to my friend, and what an experience of pleasure people may have who know anything about flowers. And it is not only one half-mile that is like this; it is many half-miles. My friend also told me of a species of buttercup not very rare, but of which in his parish he had at first found only one specimen. Year by year he went to see that specimen flower every April, and it was a pleasure to him. Gradually it increased and multiplied.

And that is another instance that so long as you do not destroy or disturb you can get pleasure in going each year, as my friend did, to see a rare plant flowering in the same place. And everyone can do so without spoiling it. The whole world of flowers and trees, of course, can be treated from the same point of view as that of birds. Then there is the whole world of insects – a very gruesome world by all accounts in some respects, but extraordinarily interesting. There is the weather, which may be of the greatest interest. I take great interest in the weather in the country. It is always some sort of a day in the country. The first thing I want to know when I wake up is what sort of a day it is. Take yesterday, the first of January, a perfect type of one sort of winter day – sun, a little frost, blue sky, and stillness the whole day. This morning I woke up to another sort of day, also attractive, cloudy, mild, and with that softness in the air which is a quality of a mild winter day. There you have two specimens of weather, each to be enjoyed in its own way, on the first two days of this year.

Then the seasons, and everything which the seasons bring with them. There is a book, a very remarkable one, written in German more than sixty years ago, I think, but translated into English, called 'On the Heights'. There is this sentence in it – a peasant woman and her husband happily married, living on their own plot of land, and one day the peasant woman is looking out of the window at the fruit trees in the orchard and she says meditatively, 'These are the trees that blossomed and bore fruit, and then the snow fell upon them, and then it was spring again.' In that one sentence there is the feeling of outdoor home. You want to be in the same place, seeing the trees and seeing the seasons passing over the same trees, seeing the first tender green of the leaf come out in April or May, and then seeing the beautiful colour of it in the autumn, and so you may multiply pleasure indefinitely. There are the stars, too, which I have not mentioned, and which have the advantage that nobody *can* destroy or disturb them. Surely the Eastern proverb comes home to us which says 'Praise Allah for the infinite diversity of his handiwork.' Books help you for the study of outdoor nature, and they are very useful in enlarging knowledge, and by enlarging knowledge you increase pleasure. For knowledge of the common English songbirds given attractively and accurately, I recommend Ward Fowler's 'A Year with the Birds'; and if you want to have the pleasures of nature expressed in the best English you will find this in Walton's 'Angler' and Gilbert White's 'Selborne'. There are also the books of the late Mr W. H. Hudson. For knowledge of many things, including the stars, probably 'The Outline of Science,' which has been coming out in parts and is, I believe, now complete, will be most valuable. Books do help, and I would quote to you two stanzas of Wordsworth which seem to me to have in them the feeling that I have been trying to express of the beauty of nature, of something which may be a joy to everyone. They are these:

> They dance not for me
> Yet mine is their glee!
> Thus pleasure is spread through the earth,
> In stray gifts to be claimed by whoever shall find,
> And a rich loving kindness, redundantly kind,
> Moves all nature to gladness and mirth.
>
> The showers of the spring
> Rouse the birds, and they sing;
> If the wind do but stir for his proper delight,
> Each leaf, that and this, his neighbours will kiss;
> Each wave, one and t'other, speeds after his brother;
> They are happy, for that is their right!

That is the 'joy in widest commonalty spread'.

Joy is not the only aspect of nature; but it is the aspect which appeals most to us; it is a very real one, and I think on the whole the dominating aspect of outdoor nature is that of pleasure and joy. There is one sentence from Jeremy Taylor that may be relevant in considering the pleasure that can be got from outdoor nature, and it is this: 'I sleep ... I drink and eat, I read and meditate, I walk in my neighbour's pleasant fields, and see all the varieties of natural beauty, I delight in that in which God delights, that is, in wisdom and virtue, and in the whole creation, and in God himself. And He that hath so many forms of joy, must needs be very much in love with sorrow and peevishness, who loseth all these pleasures, and chooseth to sit upon his little handful of thorns.'

I have quoted these things, because I think they have in them the spirit of the pleasure we get from outdoor nature if we have the capacity of taking pleasure in it. If people have not that interest in outdoor nature – birds, trees, gardens, stars, and all the rest – then let them try to find something else in which they can get as much recreation and pleasure, which is wholesome for the mind and body, and which endures and increases, as does the pleasure in outdoor nature for those who have inclination for it. If anyone shows signs of that inclination and capacity, I would say to those who teach him or her, 'By all possible means cultivate that capacity, because if you

cultivate it you will find through life that it goes on
increasing and never palls. You will be always getting
fresh interest and increasing pleasure, and in your
pleasure you will find happiness and contentment.'

LIST OF BIRDS MENTIONED

BRITISH BIRDS

Bittern *Botaurus stellaris stellaris*
Blackbird *Turdus merula merula*
Blackcap *Sylvia atracapilla*
Bluethroat, Norwegian *Luscinia svecica gaetkei*
Bramble Finch; Brambling *Fringilla montifringilla*
Bullfinch, British *Pyrrhula pyrrhula nesa*
Bunting, Cirl *Emberiza cirlus*
    "   Corn *Emberiza calandra calandra*
    "   Reed *Emberiza schoeniclus schoeniclus*
    "   Yellow Hammer *Emberiza citrinella citrinella*
Capercaillie *Tetrao urogallus urogallus*
Chaffinch *Fringilla coelebs coelebs*
Chiff-chaff *Phylloscopus collybita collybita*
Coot *Fulica atra atra*
Cormorant *Phalacrocorax carbo carbo*
Corncrake (Landrail) *Crex crex*
Crow (Carrion) *Corvus corone corone*
Cuckoo *Cuculus canorus canorus*

Curlew *Numenius arquata arquata*

Dipper (Water Ousel), British *Cinclus cinclus gularis*

Diver, Black-throated *Colymbus arcticus arcticus*

"   Great Northern *Colymbus immer*

"   Red-throated *Colymbus stellatus*

Dunnock (Hedge Sparrow), British *Prunella modularis occidentalis*

Eider Duck *Somateria mollissima mollissima*

Fieldfare *Turdus pilaris*

Flycatcher (Spotted) *Muscicapa striata striata*

Goldcrest, British *Regulus regulus anglorum*

Goldeneye *Bucephala clangula clangula*

Goldfinch, British *Carduelis carduelis britannica*

Goose, Bean *Anser fabalis fabalis*

Goose, Bernicle *Branta leucopsis*

"   Brent *Branta bernicla bernicla*

"   Grey Lag *Anser anser*

"   Pink-footed *Anser brachyrhyncha*

"   White-fronted *Anser albifrons albifrons*

Grebe, Great Crested *Podiceps cristatus cristatus*

"   Little (Dabchick) *Podiceps ruficollis ruficollis*

Greenfinch *Chloris chloris chloris*

Grouse *Lagopus scoticus scoticus*

"   Black *Lyrurux tetrix britannicus*

Guillemot (Southern) *Uria aalge albionis*

Gull, Black-headed *Larus ridibundus ridibundus*

Hawfinch *Coccothraustes coccothraustes coccothraustes*

Hawk, Sparrow *Accipiter nisus nisus*

Jackdaw *Coloeus monedula spermologus*

Kingfisher *Alcedo atthis ispida*

Knot *Calidris canutus canutus*

Lark, Sky *Alauda arvensis arvensis*

" Wood *Lullula arborea arborea*

Linnet *Carduelis cannabina cannabina*

Long-tailed Duck *Clangula hyemalis*

Mallard *Anas platyrhyncha platyrhyncha*

Martin, House *Delichon urbica urbica*

" Sand *Riparia riparia riparia*

Moorhen *Gallinula chloropus chloropus*

Nightingale *Luscinia megarhyncha megarhyncha*

Nightjar *Caprimulgus europaeus europaeus*

Nuthatch *Sitta europaea affinis*

Owl, Barn *Tyto alba alba*

" Brown *Strix aluco sylvatica*

Oyster Catcher *Haematopus ostralegus ostralegus*

Partridge *Perdix perdix perdix*

Peewit (Lapwing) *Vanellus vanellus*

Peregrine Falcon *Falco peregrinus peregrinus*

Phalarope, Red-necked *Phalaropus lobatus*

Pheasant *Phasianus colchicus*

Pintail Duck *Anas acuta acuta*

Pipit, Meadow *Anthus pratensis*

" Tree *Anthus trivialis trivialis*

Plover, Golden (Southern) *Charadrius apricarius apricarius*

Pochard, Red-crested *Netta rufina*

" Red-headed (common) *Nyroca ferina ferina*

Pochard, White-eyed *Nyroca nyroca nyroca*

Redshank *Tringa totanus totanus*

Redstart *Phoenicurus phoenicurus phoenicurus*

Redwing *Turdus musicus*

Robin, British *Erithacus rubecula melophilus*

Rook *Corvus frugilegus frugilegus*

Ruff, Reeve *Philomachus pugnax*

Sanderling *Crocethia alba*

Sandpiper, Common *Tringa hypoleucos*

       "   Curlew *Calidris testacea*

       "   Green *Tringa ochropus*

       "   Purple *Calidris maritima maritima*

Sheldrake *Tadorna tadorna*

Shoveler *Spatula clypeata*

Shrike, Great Grey *Lanius excubitor excubitor*

       "   Red-backed *Lanius collurio collurio*

Snipe, Common *Capella gallinago gallinago*

       "   Jack *Lymnocryptes minimus*

Sparrow, House *Passer domesticus domesticus*

Starling *Sturnus vulgaris vulgaris*

Stockdove *Columba enas*

Stonechat *Saxicola torquata hibernans*

Swallow *Hirundo rustica rustica*

Swan, Mute *Cygnus olor*

Swift *Apus apus apus*

Teal, Common *Anas crecca crecca*

Tern, " *Sterna hirundo hirundo*

Thicknee (Stone Curlew) *Burhinus oedicnemus oedicnemus*

Thrush, Mistle *Turdus viscivorus viscivorus*

" Song *Turdus philomelus clarkei*

Tit, Bearded *Panurus biarmicus biarmicus*

" Blue (British) *Parus coeruleus obscurus*

" Coal *Parus ater britannicus*

" Crested (Scottish) *Parus cristatus scoticus*

" Great (British) *Parus major newtoni*

" Long-tailed " *Aegithalos caudatus roseus*

" Marsh (British) *Parus palustris dresseri*

" Willow " *Parus atracapillus kleinschmidti*

Treecreeper *Certhia familiaris britannica*

Tufted Duck *Nyroca fuligula*

Turnstone *Arenaria interpres interpres*

Turtle Dove *Streptopelia turtur turtur*

Wagtail, Grey *Motacilla cinerea cinerea*

" Pied *Motacilla alba yarrellii*

Warbler, Blackcap *Sylvia atracapilla atracapilla*

" Garden *Sylvia borin*

" Grasshopper *Locustella naevia naevia*

" Reed *Acrocephalus scirpaceus scirpaceus*

" Sedge *Acrocephalus schoenolaenus*

" Willow *Phylloscopus trochilus trochilus*

" Wood *Phylloscopus sibilatrix sibilatrix*

Waxwing *Bombycilla garrulus*

Wheatear *Oenanthe oenanthe oenanthe*

Whitethroat, Common *Sylvia communis communis*

" Lesser *Sylvia corruca corruca*

Wigeon *Anas penelope*

Woodcock *Scolopax rusticola rusticola*
Woodpecker, Green *Picus viridis virescens*
     "   Larger Spotted *Dryobates major anglicus*
     "   Lesser " *Dryobates minor comminutus*
Wood-pigeon *Columba palumbus palumbus*
Wren *Troglodytes troglodytes troglodytes*

FOREIGN BIRDS

American Robin *Planesticus migratorius migratorius*
Chilian Teal *Anas flavirostre*
Chiloe Wigeon *Anas sibilatrix*
Mandarin Duck *Aix galericulata*
Peacock *Pavo cristatus*
Pintail, Chilian *Dafila spinicauda*
White-Faced Whistling Duck *Dendrocygna viduata*
Wood Duck (Carolina) *Aix sponsa*